From Red Earth

From Red Earth

A Rwandan Story of Healing and Forgiveness

Denise Uwimana

Plough Publishing House

Published by Plough Publishing House
Walden, New York
Robertsbridge, England
Elsmore, Australia
www.plough.com

Plough produces books, a quarterly magazine, and Plough.com to encourage people and help them put their faith into action. We believe Jesus can transform the world and that his teachings and example apply to all aspects of life. At the same time, we seek common ground with all people regardless of their creed.

Plough is the publishing house of the Bruderhof, an international Christian community. The Bruderhof is a fellowship of families and singles practicing radical discipleship in the spirit of the first church in Jerusalem (Acts 2 and 4). Members devote their entire lives to serving God, one another, and their neighbors, renouncing private property and sharing everything. To learn more about the Bruderhof's faith, history, and daily life, see Bruderhof.com. (Views expressed by Plough authors are their own and do not necessarily reflect the position of the Bruderhof.)

ISBN: 978-0-87486-984-2
23 22 21 20 19   1 2 3 4 5 6 7

Cover photograph by Martin Huleatt

A catalog record for this book is available from the British Library
Library of Congress Cataloging-in-Publication Data

Names: Uwimana, Denise, author.
Title: From red earth : a Rwandan story of healing and forgiveness / Denise Uwimana.
Description: [Walden, New York] : Plough Publishing House, 2019.
Identifiers: LCCN 2018056127 (print) | LCCN 2018057335 (ebook) | ISBN 9780874860023 (epub) | ISBN 9780874860450 (mobi) | ISBN 9780874862256 (pdf) | ISBN 9780874869842 (pbk.)
Subjects: LCSH: Rwanda--History--Civil War, 1994--Atrocities. | Rwanda--History--Civil War, 1994--Personal narratives. | Genocide survivors--Rwanda. | Tutsi (African people)--Crimes against--Rwanda--History--20th century. | Rwanda--Ethnic relations. | Reconciliation--Social aspects--Rwanda. | Reconciliation--Political aspects--Rwanda.
Classification: LCC DT450.437 (ebook) | LCC DT450.437 .U95 2019 (print) | DDC 967.5710431--dc23
LC record available at https://lccn.loc.gov/2018056127

Printed in the United States of America

In memory of my beloved husband Charles and all my family, friends, neighbors, and fellow Rwandans who perished in the genocide against the Tutsi.

Contents

Congo

● Gisenyi

Lake
Kivu

Idjwi
Island

● Bisesero

Nyanza ●

● Mukoma

● Kamembe
● Cyangugu

●
Bideka
school
Cimerwa ● ● Karengera
cement
factory,
Bugarama

Butare ●

Bwegera
●

Uganda

Rwanda

Ntete
Gahini
Lake
Muhazi
Kigali
Rwamagana

Tanzania

gara

Burundi

0   10   20   30 miles

I

Plane Crash

I HAVE HEARD that in the United States, people remember exactly what they were doing when planes hit the Twin Towers. In my country, too, we remember a plane crash that way. There is this difference: On September 11, nearly three thousand people died. In Rwanda, smaller in size and population than Ohio, the number was three times that many every day – for a hundred days.

Or think of it this way: if you stacked fifteen copies of this book, every word would represent one man, woman, or child murdered during the genocide against the Tutsi.

I'm trying to help people grasp what happened, because no one can picture a million human beings killed. Not even we who survived.

MY FIRST AWARENESS, when I woke on Thursday, April 7, 1994, was a too-familiar sense that the other side of the bed was flat, cold, empty. In the two and a half years since my husband had been forced to move out, I never got used to his absence. I felt it most keenly after one of his clandestine visits, like the one the previous weekend.

I missed Charles now more than ever. For the last six months, tension had been mounting in our town, Bugarama. With all the bad news and rumors, a heavy dread had been growing within me. This was bad, because a child was growing within me too. Our baby was due to be born in just two weeks.

I yearned to put my head under the pillow, pretend life was normal, and go back to sleep. But that was not an option. My two little sons relied on me. So did two young cousins – Aline, fifteen, and Thérèse, sixteen – who had been sent by my uncles to keep me company. Our houseboy, Samuel, lived with us as well; in Rwandan society, every middle-class family had a teenage boy or girl to help with chores and shopping. I could count on him to make breakfast, yet he, too, seemed an overgrown child.

An internal poke – my baby's elbow? or heel? – was the nudge I needed to pull myself out of bed and get going with the day. Standing at the window, combing my hair into a frizz around my head, I looked over our front yard, edged by its high fence and iron gate, to Cimerwa's cement plant – our factory town's reason for existence – across the road.

Lifting my eyes from the industrial scene, I rested them on the hazy mountains bounding my view. Charles was beyond that horizon. Doing my hair the way he liked it was my tiny act of defiance against the company directors who had forced him to leave home.

The sky was lightening above the hills. I put down my pick and switched on the radio to catch the six o'clock news. But all I got this time was classical music. It droned on and on . . . no news, no announcements, not even the recent vitriol about "exterminating cockroaches."

Something was weird, and my uneasiness increased when the music continued to whine while I dressed. As the only adult in our home, I had to know what was up. I would ask Goretti, I decided. Her husband, Viateur, was Cimerwa's head mechanic, and he might have heard something.

I had known Goretti since soon after my arrival in Bugarama as a bride, seven years earlier. When I later moved into the house next to hers, she and I became best friends. Now she, too, was about to have a baby – it was eleven years since her last – and we had both taken our bassinets out of storage, in anticipation, and packed our suitcases for the hospital. Goretti liked to knit, so she'd made sweaters for our infants while I appliquéd traditional designs on their *ingobyi*, the cloths we African mothers use for carrying young children on our backs. Everything was ready . . . But now?

Before leaving the house, I peeked into my children's room. Christian lay sprawled on his back, snoring softly. He looked so peaceful, asleep; it would be a different story the moment he woke. At eighteen months, he had a toddler's knack for bumps and tumbles. Charles-Vital was curled protectively beside him in the bed they shared. A serious little thinker, my four-year-old was interested in everything, asking "why?" all day long. Normally, I savored gazing at my sleeping sons. Today, I gave them scarcely a glance before slipping out the back door.

As every morning, cocks were crowing and the dawn breeze carried the wood-smoke tang of breakfast fires. But I heard no exchange of cheery greetings, no banter, no snatches of song. I hurried through my backyard toward my neighbor's, calling her name.

Goretti appeared immediately at her back door and hastened to meet me. As she leaned on the fence separating our places, I was alarmed at the hopeless expression in her eyes. Seeing the question in mine, she took a shuddering breath.

"President Habyarimana was assassinated last night," Goretti said heavily. "His jet was shot down. He was about to land back home in Kigali."

The dread in my stomach cramped into a knot. Our president, dead in a crumpled and burning plane, had been Hutu.

I had no idea who had committed the crime. According to investigations years later, the fatal missile was almost certainly fired by Hutu extremists. But that Thursday morning, all I knew was that – without a doubt – we Tutsi would pay.

My worst forebodings, however, did not come close to the nightmare before us. It never crossed my mind that this day, April 7, was the chosen launch date for the systematic slaughter of Rwanda's Tutsi population. Yes, this was Day One of our country's Hundred Days in Hell, which would hit Bugarama on Day Nine.

The morning was cloudless, unusual for rainy April, but no sunshine could brighten my thoughts as I stumbled home to wake the children. While I helped my little sons get dressed, my mind was far away.

What will happen next? Oh Charles, I can't even contact you! How will I get to the hospital to have the baby?

After breakfast I hid my official documents under my pillow, with money I had borrowed from Cimerwa for the upcoming birth. I had no clear idea of what to do but wanted to be ready for anything. I tried to tidy the house, but found it impossible to focus.

Hearing a commotion a few hours later, I looked out the front window to see a group of rowdy factory workers coming along the road. They stopped in front of my house, and I ducked out of sight. The men started shouting obscenities as they shook my gate, fortunately still locked from the night. I recognized one of them by his voice: Wasi Wasi, who made cement sacks with my cousin Manasseh. He had always hated Tutsi.

"Hey, Denise," Wasi Wasi bellowed, "do you think you're better than Madame Agathe? You'll meet the same fate. Your time has come!"

What was he talking about? Agathe Uwilingiyimana was our Hutu prime minister, second to the president. She had courageously condemned recent murders of Tutsi. Had something happened to her?

Around noon my husband's brother Anselm and my cousin Manasseh unexpectedly showed up. They no longer felt safe in their lodgings, they explained when I let them in, and my house had a strong gate and metal doors; might they join me? I welcomed their presence and gave them the guest room. In the event of danger, they would be more dependable than young Samuel.

The next time I turned on the radio, we six adults and teenagers clustered around it to hear the news. Every announcement compounded our fear. Tutsi had shot down the president's Falcon-50 aircraft, the radio declared, and the government was imposing a curfew: no Tutsi could travel or even leave home. There would be a month of mourning for President Habyarimana, during which all manufacture was prohibited.

That meant no work at Cimerwa. My mind flashed an alarming image of hundreds of Hutu youth loose on Bugarama's streets, instead of producing cement.

The newscaster continued. At ten o'clock this morning, Madame Agathe Uwilingiyimana and her husband had been shot to death outside their home. He did not mention what I learned later – that the ten UN peacekeepers guarding them had been killed as well, after being horribly mutilated.

I switched off the radio and looked at the people who had joined me in my home. So we were under "curfew" and could not leave the house. I had no desire to step out into the madness descending on our world anyway. I closed all the curtains. It was a relief to know I had a good supply of rice, beans, and sugar in the house. I had just stocked up the week before, preparing for my baby's arrival.

In the evening, Hutu friends stopped by to report that militia were roving the area. Dizzy with worry, yet sticking to routine for my children's sake, I tucked the two little boys into bed and locked the house for the night.

When I tuned the radio to RTLM next morning, a fanatical voice was announcing an order "from the top" that the hour had come for all "snakes and cockroaches" to die. "Look in the bushes!" the voice screamed. "Look in the swamps! Wherever you find Tutsi, kill! Kill without mercy!" He named specific "enemies and traitors" to be targeted first and ended with a shriek: "The mass graves are still half-empty! Fill them up!"

From my window, for months, I had watched young men on the factory grounds in the early mornings: running, exercising, or practicing with grenades and rifles. They belonged to Interahamwe, meaning "we who attack together." These Hutu youth were recruited countrywide in their thousands, taught to hate, and trained to kill. Most wore no uniform, and many were unemployed; yet they were organized and powerful, and they had links to the national army. So I knew the crazy words coming from the radio were no empty threat.

I did not know, however, that the trained Interahamwe were now being joined countrywide by volunteer militias consisting of thugs, volunteers from nearby countries, and our own neighbors and coworkers – any Hutu who would join the massacre.

Their plan was efficient. Working from locally compiled lists, they hunted from one Tutsi home to the next, searching under beds, above ceilings, in closets and cupboards. Even dresser drawers were checked for infants. They set guards on every road and pathway to prevent escape. They scoured fields, plantations, woods, marshes, streambeds, wasteland, inside vehicles. It was the swiftest genocide in history.

Ten years later, in her book *Conspiracy to Murder,* Linda Melvern would write that "Rwanda, one of the poorest countries in the world, became the third largest importer of weapons in Africa, spending an estimated US $112 million." Interahamwe were armed with these weapons from France, Israel, Belgium, China, Egypt, South Africa, and possibly other countries as well. Many secrets remain hidden to this day. Unhidden, however, were preparations in the streets and markets. I had seen my Hutu neighbors get their machetes, in broad daylight, from the company canteen across the road.

People may wonder why we didn't try to escape, with death looming over us. They may as well ask why the mouse cowers, quivering, under scanty grass blades while the bird of prey hovers overhead. Why doesn't the little creature make a dash for safety? Maybe he knows the razor talons and flesh-tearing beak are waiting for just that, daring him to come into the open . . . Maybe he doesn't want to exchange fear in familiar surroundings for unknown terror.

We stayed where we were, my mind replaying its despairing reel: I had no way to protect my children from impending peril, nowhere safe for my baby to be born.

2

Roots

MY LIFE WAS MARKED by the conflict between Hutu and Tutsi even before I was born.

In the West, people often ask about the animosity between the two groups. Its roots are in our country's history; even among us Rwandans, there was disagreement and confusion for years due to differing versions of our past.

I asked my husband's mother, Consoletia, to clarify our history for me, because she lived through much of it herself. She answered that when Hutu extremists gained power in the late 1950s, as our country was moving toward independence, they introduced a theory that Tutsi were a separate tribe whose ancestors had come up the Nile.

"In my youth, there was no tribal distinction between Hutu and Tutsi; it was just an economic and social distinction," my mother-in-law explained. "Anyone with ten or more cows was considered Tutsi, and those who worked the fields were Hutu. A person might move from one class to the other if he gained or lost

LET US KNOW WHAT YOU THINK

VISIT **WWW.MYBKEXPERIENCE.COM**
COMPLETE OUR SURVEY **IN THE NEXT 48 HOURS**
IT'S BRIEF I PROMISE

YOU'LL GET A VALIDATION CODE, JUST WRITE IT DOWN
HERE: _____. THEN, RETURN ME TO A PARTICIPATING
BURGER KING® RESTAURANT. YOU'LL ALSO NEED TO PURCHASE A
S/M/L SIZE DRINK AND REQUIRED SIDE AT REGULAR PRICE.

ENJOY YOUR FREE *WHOPPER*® SANDWICH**

CHECK OUT THE RULES:

FOOD PURCHASE REQUIRED AND RESTRICTIONS MAY APPLY. VALIDATED RECEIPT
GOOD FOR ONE MONTH FROM DATE OF PURCHASE. NOT VALID WITH ANY OTHER
OFFER. NOT AVAILABLE TO EMPLOYEES OR THEIR FAMILIES. ONE SURVEY PER
GUEST PER MONTH. CASH VALUE 1/100¢.

"WHOPPER®SANDWICH 9487
(WITH FRIES AND SODA ONLY)

OR **ORIGINAL CHICKEN SANDWICH** 9494
(WITH FRIES AND SODA ONLY)

OR **CROISSAN'WICH**® 9500
(WITH HASHBROWNS AND COFFEE ONLY)

BURGER KING® **FREE WHOPPER**®
*FOOD PURCHASE REQUIRED

LET US KNOW WHAT YOU THINK

VISIT **WWW.MYBKEXPERIENCE.COM**
COMPLETE OUR SURVEY **IN THE NEXT 48 HOURS**
IT'S BRIEF I PROMISE

YOU'LL GET A VALIDATION CODE, JUST WRITE IT DOWN
HERE: _____. THEN, RETURN ME TO A PARTICIPATING
BURGER KING® RESTAURANT. YOU'LL ALSO NEED

Burger King ®
#11915

128 Tremont Street
Boston, MA 02108
617-556-8299

▌▐ORDER▐24▌▐

TAKE OUT

FREE 4PC NUGGETS w/pur	0.00
*CHK NUGGETS 4PC	
honey must sauce	
$5 WHOPPER MEAL	5.00
*WHOPPER	
*SM FRY	
*SM COKE	

SUBTOTAL	5.00
7% TAX	0.35
TOTAL	5.35
CREDIT CARD	5.35
CHANGE	0.00

****

TOTAL CHARGE   5.35

VISA
AcctNum: ***********9539
Auth: 040913
Type: CREDIT
CTroutd: 74493
Merchant Id: 466162542991

RETAIN THIS COPY FOR YOUR RECORDS
CUSTOMER COPY
****

Survey Code: 51211-34111-04903-190522

===================================
WHOPPER® SANDWICH FOR YOUR THOUGHT:
www.mybkexperience.com
CHECK ON BACK FOR FOOD OFFER.
OUR GOAL IS YOUR SATISFACTION!
===================================
Mon Nov 04 2019 03:08 PM T=01_ I=2 C=182

wealth – there was social mobility both ways. As a child, I knew a family where one brother was Hutu and another was Tutsi. In any case, we shared the same language and culture, and intermarriage was common throughout the country. It was the Europeans who invented an 'ethnic difference' between us."

Germany claimed Rwanda as a colony in 1895, as part of German East Africa. From the beginning, these Europeans favored the Tutsi minority, wanting to stay in league with the royal family and upper class. Belgium, which took over in 1916 during the First World War, at first continued this pro-Tutsi policy, offering our people careers and Western-style education. The Hutu majority naturally resented this discrimination. I am certain the colonists deliberately sowed division and envy in order to control the population more easily.

In 1933, Belgium decreed that every man and woman had to carry an ID card stating their "ethnicity." In cases of mixed parentage, a person's identity would be that of the father. Ethnic role call was introduced in schools; all Tutsi pupils, or all Hutu, would be told to stand up, so the teacher could see who was who.

Realizing that power was shifting to the vocal majority, Belgium suddenly switched its preference in 1959. So by the time our country gained independence in 1962, free at last from European domination, the reins of the new government were firmly in Hutu hands. That's when my parents fled the country, which is why I was born in Burundi.

My parents were certainly not the only Tutsi to leave Rwanda. There were two major waves of violence in a fifteen-year period, during which approximately 300,000 escaped to neighboring countries: Uganda, Tanzania, Burundi, and the Congo. The Hutu government forbade these Rwandans to come home. It's important to understand this, because the Rwandan Patriotic Front, which later played a crucial role, was mobilized from among these exiles.

MY FATHER, SIMEON Muganga Rugema, was born in 1937. He grew up with six brothers and sisters on his parents' farm, near Karengera, in western Rwanda. He left home for a couple of years to train as a nurse, then returned to help support the family.

As a young man, partying with friends was his idea of having a good time; and when he and my mother were getting acquainted, they quarreled about how much he spent on drink. Religion was not particularly important to my father back then. He went to church once a week, mainly to sing and socialize.

In 1960, however, he attended an evangelistic campaign in Bujumbura, led by Billy Graham. That was my father's turning point; from then on, life became a matter of putting his faith into action, moment by moment. He married my mother on April 4, 1962.

My mother's name was Kampogo Joyce, but my father called her Mwiza, "beautiful one." Our neighbors called her Karibu Kwangu, "welcome to my home," to reflect her generous spirit. Unlike my father, she never even learned to read. She had spent her childhood walking the hills overlooking Lake Kivu, with her family's dairy herd. Rwandan cattle look nothing like milk cows in Europe or America – docile but massive, they have curved horns that can span six feet. My mother knew just where to take them to find the richest grass at every season. She also knew the name and personality of each cow in her care.

Although Hutu made up eighty-five percent of Rwanda's population, the region around my mother's village, Muramba, was almost entirely Tutsi. For my mother's extended family and their neighbors, life moved to the rhythm of morning and evening milking. As long as they had cattle, they could nourish their families with milk, butter, and *mashanja*, our version of yogurt.

Each cow was treasured, and giving one away was a statement of lasting friendship. If my grandfather wanted to emphasize the truth of his word, he would name someone who had given him a cow. On the rare occasions when one was slaughtered – before a wedding, for example – every part of the animal was used: meat, leather, organs, and horns. The groom's family presenting cattle to the bride's family is still an elaborate part of marriage festivities in our culture.

What my mother lacked in formal education, she compensated for in natural wisdom and common sense. My earliest memory is of several somber adults looking down at me. I was five, I was in bed, and I had measles – frequently fatal in East Africa back then. But my recollection of measles is a happy one, because Mama brought chocolate milk and sat beside me, recounting her childhood adventures and reciting humorous poems she had composed as a girl while watching her family's cows.

Although my parents were so different from each other – or perhaps because they were so different – they were a great match. We three daughters and six sons never witnessed their earlier strife but only how they worked together to raise us and to care for their neighbors. I remember my father praying that they might live to celebrate fifty years of marriage. His wish was granted in 2012, when our family gathered from several continents to celebrate their golden wedding anniversary. My mother even recited one of her old poems for the occasion, about a recalcitrant cow.

3
Refugee Childhood

MY PARENTS VIEWED the date of my birth as a good omen. December 13 was the third Sunday of Advent in 1964, the day they lit three candles out of four in expectation of Christ's birthday. I was their second child, and the first daughter.

Kibuye Hospital, where I was born, had been built twenty years earlier by American Methodist missionaries to Burundi. Since Papa was on the hospital staff, our home – a solid brick house with wood beams and tiled roof – was part of the mission compound, as were the church and school.

Thanks to an altitude of six thousand feet, Kibuye's climate is idyllic, and we children spent our days outdoors. My older brother Phocas and I often climbed avocado, orange, and guava trees. We would pick and eat the fruit or just enjoy our leafy world, above the rest of the human race.

At bedtime, we pestered Mama for stories of her childhood. While we huddled under our covers, she would describe volcanoes on Idjwi Island and on Lake Kivu's far Congo shore. As a young girl, she had seen their glow reflected from the clouds at night.

Sometimes our mother stretched her memories, to describe demon-people and their offspring living in the fiery cones – stirring clay pots in the smoldering heat, eating the seething contents, laughing, singing, and spewing lava over the land. It was too dark to see the smile in Mama's eyes – night comes quickly at the equator – but I heard it in her voice. I shivered happily under my blanket and begged for more.

When I was nearly six, I started school, setting off in my blue uniform like the twenty-nine other first graders. I could hardly wait to make the mysterious marks on paper that I had watched my older brother create. Dashing home a few hours later, I took some chalk and proudly demonstrated my new letters and numerals on our concrete floor.

When my parents were out of the room, Phocas helped me get down the heavy Bible. Cross-legged on the floor, I opened it and started dissecting letters from words, eager to read at last. But there was no meaning! Disgruntled, I told my brother to put the book away. This education business would take some time.

My parents were fluent in Kirundi, the language of our adopted country. That's what we kids used for talking with our playmates, our teachers, and each other. But when they didn't want us to understand their conversation, our parents switched to Kinyarwanda, their mother tongue – so our ears became fine-tuned to that as well. The two languages are quite similar.

When I was seven, my family packed our belongings and left the only home I knew. I didn't understand why, but again the reason was Hutu–Tutsi strife. Following a 1972 uprising, Tutsi leaders in Burundi incited the killing of thousands of Hutu. We saw none of this violence in our village, and our parents never discussed it in front of us children – but they decided it was time to leave the country.

My father accepted his uncle Sekabarata's invitation to Kaziba, in the Congo, to pursue further studies at a teaching hospital there. Only six years older than Papa, Sekabarata seemed more like a brother than an uncle to my father. Years earlier, they had undertaken their initial nursing training together.

The journey to Kaziba was an adventure for us kids – five of us now. After crossing the Ruzizi River, which separates Burundi from the Congo, we boarded the truck that would take us to our new home. Papa hoisted me onto its tailgate, and I pressed my way forward.

I hoped to cling to a side of the vehicle, to have a secure handhold and watch the scenery. Instead, as at least thirty others clambered aboard, I found my face mashed into the back of a large lady. All I could see was the swirling pattern of her cotton *kitenge*, the African wrap-around skirt. Just when I was sure I would suffocate between strangers, I felt a firm touch on my shoulder. It was Mama, reassuring me through the press.

The road's deep ruts, formed during the rainy season and hardened like rock, made our vehicle lurch violently. Only our packed condition prevented me from falling over. For one stretch, the road led through mountains, with a cliff falling from its edge. I could not see this drop-off or the swamp hundreds of feet below, but the passengers' outbursts fueled my imagination. Every time the truck tilted, I was sure it would plunge us all into the Nkombo Chasm.

After six hours of standing in the truck, our family arrived, exhausted but safe, in Kaziba, our new home deep in the Congo. Uncle Sekabarata told us we could stay in his house until the mission would provide our own.

Despite my great-uncle's hearty welcome, I felt like an alien in the Congo. Kaziba's population belonged to the Bashi tribe and spoke an unfamiliar tongue. School lessons were held in French and Swahili, two more languages my brothers and I had to master.

Being refugees and strangers was challenging for our parents, too, until matters took a fortuitous turn.

The mountains surrounding Kaziba are home to the Banyamulenge, a proud people who measure their wealth by the size of their cattle herds. Although they have been in the Congo more than four hundred years, they originally came from what is now Rwanda, and they speak a form of Kinyarwanda similar to ours.

The Banyamulenge we came to know walked barefoot with dignity, the men in long coats and felt hats – cane in hand, to guide their lethal-looking cows through rocky terrain – the women fully draped, showing only their eyes. Their families would come down from the mountains to Kaziba for medical treatment, or to send their children to school, selling cattle to pay the fees. Uncle Sekabarata always welcomed the Banyamulenge. The house we shared with him smelled rancid whenever he hosted them, because they used butter both for cooking and as lotion.

The Banyamulenge salute – *Uri uwo kwande muntu?*, "Who do you belong to?" – led to our breakthrough. In answering this greeting, Papa discovered that we were distantly related to some of these folk. We had known we were linked by a shared past, but it was exciting to realize we had specific ancestors in common. Weary of being foreigners, my parents decided to join the Banyamulenge tribe. That's how we freed ourselves from our refugee status and became citizens of the Congo.

Years later Mama, in true African style, arranged a match for me – with a Banyamulenge man. My siblings joked that she was inspired by her love of cattle, because she and Papa would have gained twelve cows from the transaction.

Sometimes I try to picture what my life might have been, had I agreed to her plan. I would probably be weaving cloth for my husband's coat right now, or cooking over the fire in the center of a round mud hut, my shins burned from squatting too near the flames. Or maybe I'd be smearing my children with butter . . . The only certainty is that life would have been far more serene than it turned out.

After completing his training at Kaziba Hospital, my father was assigned by the mission to direct a health center in Kalambi, a village in the Congo's eastern borderland. That meant another move. I was ten.

Kalambi turned out to be a primitive jungle community. Once again, everything was unfamiliar. Only the few houses belonging to the mission, including ours, had brick walls and metal roofs. The other homes, on both sides of a central dirt road, were built of mud and thatched with straw.

People going to the health center had to pass our house, and they often stopped in for a drink of water. Mama always gave visitors something to eat as well, especially the pregnant mothers. And as clinic director, Papa would go out at a moment's notice, day or night, to deal with any accident, snakebite, birth, or death. In this way, my parents quickly gained the respect of most of the villagers.

Making friends was harder for us kids. We were the first foreigners the village children had ever seen, and they asked, in a mocking chant, which planet we were from. They despised my older brother when he stayed away from their manhood initiation rites. They eventually accepted us, however, when they saw that we could run and joke like them. They belonged to various tribes – Barega, Banyindu, Babembe, and Twa – and we gradually picked up their dialects.

Kalambi's population lived mainly by subsistence farming, cassava being the staple crop. People also raised fish in manmade ponds and harvested food from the forest. A large spiny caterpillar, *milanga*, was a popular source of protein.

The first time Phocas, my younger brother Clement, and I saw *milanga* on the trees, we could not believe they were edible. As long as a man's finger, and much fatter, this red-brown larva was covered with spikes. However scary they were to look at – and painful to pick up – collecting them in season was a gala event for the village. Mama said eating caterpillars was disgusting, and she forbade us to bring *milanga* into our house. On my own, however, I discovered how tasty they were.

My best friend Bishoshi, two years older than I, lived in the brick house next to ours. Her mother Marthe was a midwife who worked in the clinic with my father. I admired Bishoshi and spent most of my time with her. So when she offered me batter-fried *milanga* in her home, I enjoyed it without a qualm.

In October, and again in March, flocks of birds made shifting patterns across Kalambi's sky. When they landed in the village trees, I saw that they were drab little birds – but I liked them. Decades later, in Europe, I recognized my small friends and realized they had visited us in Africa to escape their wintry homelands. I couldn't blame them.

There was no lack of warmth in our steamy world. We would look out first thing in the morning to see nothing but thick white mist, which would disperse a couple hours later to reveal the dripping rainforest surrounding the village. There were regal palms and graceful bamboo, magenta bougainvillea, and lush undergrowth. Small yellow stars dotted the grass along the jungle's edge. Brilliant butterflies flitted over these flowers or landed on the track to suck moisture from the mud. The place looked like paradise.

It was a dangerous paradise, however. As well as gorgeous blossoms, there were barbed thorns, stinging insects, and a bush that caused a painful, itchy rash if you accidentally brushed its leaves. Worse, any verdant vine or fern could hide a deadly snake. The villagers stored herbs to treat certain kinds of snakebite, but they warned that there was no remedy for others. We occasionally saw cobras, but most common were green mambas, slithering up tree trunks or draped in the branches.

One morning when I was eleven, I opened the outhouse door – and screamed. But I couldn't move a muscle. An eight-foot black mamba was coiled on the cool earth floor. This species is actually gray or brown, but the inside of its mouth, revealed when it gives its warning hiss, is a threatening black.

Hearing my scream, my father's brother Ezra – visiting from Rwanda – came running with a hoe and killed the snake. He and I were incredibly lucky. Feared for both their speed and the potency of their venom, black mambas kill hundreds of people in the Congo every year. Much later, though, I couldn't help wondering: Would Ezra have preferred death by snakebite to the death he suffered at the hands of fellow human beings?

Because of the snakes, we children never climbed trees here as we had in Burundi, nor were we allowed to explore the mysterious jungle, from which we heard raucous birdcalls by day and eerie cries at night. So, to our disappointment, we could never see the monkeys at play in the treetops. One day, however, a man showed us the paw of a gorilla he had killed deep in the forest. I shuddered. The powerful paw was bigger than the man's hand.

Like other village children, my brothers and I herded goats, collected firewood, fetched water, and tended our family crops. Phocas and Clement cleared brush with machetes, while I cultivated with a heavy hoe or pulled weeds by hand. Our father's young sister Priscilla, who lived with us at the time, often helped.

Reaching the end of a cassava row one day, I was startled when a thick, mottled creeper – spiraled around a bamboo trunk at the field's edge – began to slide. Glancing up, I met the glittering eyes of a python. I knew they killed by encircling their prey, tightening their muscular bodies till its bones cracked. Dropping my hoe, I fled the field.

Next day, on the way to our plot I burst out, "Let's ask God to protect us!" Priscilla said a prayer, and that day we were spared the sight of snakes.

The four youngest children in our family were born in Kalambi, and our mother depended on my help at home. Our biggest task was processing cassava. With long knives, we peeled the roots and placed them, tied in cloth, into the creek to soften – and to get rid of their bitter flavor. Three days later, we took the roots from the water and laid them in the sun. When they were dry, we pounded them into flour, which we stirred into boiling water. The result was *ugari*, a filling starch that we served with fish sauce or vegetables.

I helped clean the house, hauled water, ran errands for my father, and looked after Fidel – my eight-years-younger brother – carrying him everywhere on my hip or on my back. A tall man now, Fidel likes to tease me, saying he's the reason I'm so short.

When we weren't helping our mothers, we girls contented ourselves playing hopscotch and other games in the village street. Needing some way to cool off, we often swam in the fish ponds – although this was forbidden, and the mud smelled foul – or waded and splashed in the creek.

Before returning home from an afternoon at the creek, Bishoshi and I would catch crabs for our mothers to cook, shrieking with laughter if one of us was careless enough to get pinched. We never spared a thought for the black stones under which the crabs hid. Only years later did prospectors discover our streambed rocks, which turned out to be valuable columbite, coveted for manufacture of electronic products.

In 1977, when I was twelve, Papa took Phocas, Clement, and me to visit his own parents in Rwanda. We had never met our grandfather, Ephraim. But we knew our grandmother, Damaris, because she had come to spend time with our family in Kalambi. I admired Tateh Damaris when I learned of the risk she had taken to visit us in the Congo; as a Tutsi, she might not have been allowed back into Rwanda.

Now the time had come to see her again and to meet Tateh Ephraim. I was thrilled. I would see the mighty Lake Kivu – thirty miles across at its widest, and fifty-six miles long – that Mama was always reminiscing about. And I would finally experience Rwanda, land of my ancestors, country of a thousand hills.

The first thing I noticed, on arrival in my grandparents' village, was the red earth, so different from Kalambi's black soil. Like us, our grandparents grew cassava, sorghum, coffee, soy beans, potatoes, and yams on their farm. But they also raised fruit near their house: banana, papaya, guava, and pineapple. They kept livestock too. They were quite wealthy.

Tateh Damaris rose early to prepare breakfast for her family and for the farm hands. During our month's stay, I helped her tidy the house, grounds, livestock paddock, and paths. Next we would spread rushes on the floor, then feed the hens and gather their eggs. I walked the pastureland, collecting cakes of dry cow dung for fuel. In a large flat basket, I collected fresh dung as well, which Tateh Damaris and I plastered on the house walls as weatherproofing.

Phocas, Clement, and I revered Tateh Ephraim; after all, he was Papa's father. A deep thinker, he enjoyed sharing his wisdom through maxims, jokes, and proverbs. "Do evil when good no longer exists on the earth," he would tell us. We knew he meant: Do only good.

During the day, our grandfather tended his cattle, sheep, and goats. In the evening, he herded them into their enclosure, pulling thorny branches across its opening as protection from predators.

Seeing a mass of fish in a large crock one day, I happily anticipated a fish fry, such as we occasionally enjoyed in Kalambi. To my shock, however, Tateh Ephraim started hoeing the fish into the ground in his banana grove. His explanation – that fish made good fertilizer – startled me, but I never doubted him. His crops were excellent.

Although Tateh Ephraim had never been to school, he had taught himself to read. When his day's work was done, he put on the pair of glasses Papa had sent him, relaxed into his comfortable chair, and read his Bible. One evening he called me to his side.

"Scripture says hard times will come over the earth in the last days, my child," he said. "People will change their ways for the worse."

Another time he remarked, "When I read the Bible in Kinyarwanda, I understand it best. Kinyarwanda is the most beautiful language in the world!" I avoided Clement's eye, afraid we might burst out laughing. Kinyarwanda was the only language our grandfather knew.

Sundays we joined our grandparents on their forty-five minute walk to church in Karengera. Tateh Damaris, a woman of style, wore an elegant *mushanana*. Usually kept for rare celebrations, this traditional garment is tied at one shoulder and falls in graceful folds to the ankle. Along our way, we had to traverse some rickety planks over a swirling creek. While I hesitated, my dignified grandmother traipsed confidently across in her high heels. I felt proud to see how respectfully my grandparents were greeted by everyone we met along the way – Hutu, Tutsi, and Twa.

4

Wakening

MY FATHER'S FAITH shaped our family's outlook. Through daily example, he and Mama taught us children to love our friends and neighbors – and enemies – and to trust in God, no matter what.

The way Papa described a coming kingdom of peace and justice, I expected to wake up to it any morning. I would peek outside, hoping to glimpse a leopard romping with a baby goat, or a lion eating straw like an ox. My mind stopped short, however, at the idea of my baby brother putting his hand into a viper's nest. Shuddering, I turned my imagination away from snakes.

Singing was as natural as eating in our home. Since Papa could read music, he often taught us songs from his Kirundi and Swahili songbooks. His favorite, picked up at the Billy Graham crusade – *Mbega urukundo ry'Imana yacu,* "How great is God's love, beyond all telling" – accompanied us through the years.

Every evening, we gathered in the living room to sing, pray, and listen to Papa's Bible stories. He described a father scanning the horizon for his disobedient son – then running to embrace him when he returned home, ashamed, after disgracing the family. He told about a good shepherd who left his large herd in their enclosure to search for one lost lamb, in danger from eagles by day and hyenas at night. He spoke of a disciple who could walk on water as long as he kept his eyes on Jesus.

Christmas was my favorite time of year. Then Papa told about Mary, a young girl like me, and about an angel telling her she would become mother to the best baby in the world. He described hosts of angels proclaiming her child's birth, in song, to herders on the hillside at night. But he also spoke of great hardships: that although the baby had been announced by heaven and honored with gold and incense, he had to flee for his life, a refugee with his parents, while soldiers slaughtered the infant boys of Bethlehem. And when he grew up, he was killed, suffering a cruel death out of love for us all. It was more than I could understand. But I knew I loved this child above everything.

Part of our evening ritual was apologizing for any offense of the day. For me, that usually meant making peace with Clement, with whom I fought most. One day I told the whole family I was sorry for grabbing the core when Mama cut up our pineapple – but that didn't prevent my grabbing the neck when she carved our roast chicken the next day.

In the evening prayer, Papa asked God to heal our mother, who was often unwell. We prayed for alcoholics in our village. We asked for protection from illness – malaria plagued the region – and from evil powers. We also prayed for our father's work in the hospital, especially for the pregnant women, since mothers sometimes died in childbirth.

One day a baby was born beside the road outside our village, and Papa was called to help. At the end of that week when, as always, our father asked each of us what to thank God for, my sister Rose told him to give thanks for the baby born at the roadside. I always wanted him to thank God that none of us had been bitten by a snake.

Our evening gathering gave me security to face the nights, which were utterly dark in this place of no electricity. Kalambi was ruled by superstition, and most local Barega wore amulets to ward off evil. The scream of a jungle cat foretold bad luck, the villagers said, and you would die if you answered a night bird's call. Even when someone died of malaria, the death was blamed on magic.

A neighbor whispered to Mama that local sorceresses had killed their own husbands. Mama did not know if this was true, and did not want to know. But when weird sounds woke me in the darkness, or I remembered the neighbors' dire stories and predictions, I reassured myself back to sleep with one of Papa's songs.

As I grew into adolescence, I continued to spend time with my best friend, Bishoshi, and her mother, Marthe. I wasn't the only one at their house. All the kids enjoyed Bishoshi's cheery, outgoing ways. She seemed to be always preparing and serving food.

One morning while we were eating breakfast, Marthe burst into our house. "Bishoshi is very sick!" she cried. "I can't wake her!"

Papa hurried out. I pushed my food away, my appetite replaced by a knot of anxiety.

Bishoshi's condition was too critical for Kalambi's health center, so Papa drove her to the hospital in Mwenga. On return, he told us Bishoshi had meningitis and explained how serious it was.

A week later she died. She was fourteen.

Losing my best friend was terrible, inconceivable, and I could not stop crying. My parents told me Bishoshi was with God, but that seemed a remote idea. It was my first close encounter with death. How could Bishoshi be alive and laughing one week, and gone forever the next? I was also frightened: if death could take her, what about me?

In the evening, after Papa told us the news, my siblings and I went to Marthe's house next door. She welcomed us, and she seemed to take comfort from seeing that we shared her grief, so we kept returning. Others joined us. Every day the group of children and teenagers grew.

Over the next couple of weeks, as we continued to meet in Marthe's house – where I still sensed Bishoshi's nearness – my heaviness began to lift. I found myself eagerly anticipating our next gathering. And as we sang, prayed, and read the Bible together, a greater joy than I had ever known welled up in my heart. I had never given heaven much thought before, but now it seemed real, natural, and close. The others felt the same way.

One of my friends and I prayed together in Marthe's backyard. We asked God to show us what displeased him in us – and at that moment, I remembered my quick temper. I decided to fast, to eat nothing for a couple of days, because I knew from experience that good resolutions alone would not conquer my moods. I sensed God was helping me, and that made me glad. I stopped fighting with my brothers and sisters, and I obeyed my parents more readily – not because they demanded more, but because of the peace and happiness I felt inside.

When the adults in church realized we kids were serious about giving our lives to God, they assigned a teacher to support us. They also gave us a room in the mission compound to use for our meetings. We always sang when we got together. Soon nearby villages started inviting our youth group to sing for them too.

I prayed in private now, no longer depending solely on our family devotions. I started reading the Bible myself as well, finding within it everything I thirsted for. Its last section troubled me, however. There I read that one bowl of wrath after another would be poured over the earth, and still the people would not repent. Would I experience such a "bowl of wrath" in my lifetime? It was a fearsome thought, and I decided to leave that part of the Bible until I was strong enough to handle it.

I turned thirteen during this children's revival and requested baptism. Following a brief preparation course, I was baptized on Christmas Eve, 1977.

KALAMBI HAD NO high school. So when I finished eighth grade in 1978, my parents sent me to Lycée Bideka, a Christian girls' boarding school with an excellent reputation.

Papa had earlier hoped I might become a nurse, to assist him in his work. But he and Mama realized the futility of this dream when I freaked out at the sight of blood after a child gashed his leg falling from a tree. So my parents suggested I train as a teacher. Gaining a diploma after six years at Lycée Bideka would qualify me to teach elementary school.

Although Bideka was only fifty miles from Kalambi, I rarely went home. The trip, in an open truck with thirty or forty others plus a load of freight, could take up to three days in the rainy season.

These were mind-stretching, enjoyable years. But it was at Lycée Bideka that I first encountered hatred between Hutu and Tutsi. Initially there was no division among us. I made friends with girls from Rwanda, Burundi, and different regions of Zaire, as the Congo was called during this period.

Since five of us shared the name *Uwimana* –"belonging to God"–the others renamed us to differentiate. I was *La Petite Uwimana,* because of my short stature. My classmates admired my hair, which is unusually soft. Some of them combed it out into what Westerners had started calling an afro.

When we performed dramas, my role was to sing behind the curtains. Some of our productions were hilarious, although they weren't meant to be. We laughed till we cried, seeing girls act the parts of wise men in the nativity play.

One lunchtime, the head girl was indignant to discover insects in our beans and pebbles in the rice. "Our parents pay a lot of money for us to attend this school," she declared, "and this is the food we get?" When she initiated a hunger strike, everyone enthusiastically joined in. Our three-day demonstration was good fun – and the food improved as a result.

Then some new students came from Rwanda. Since they needed help with their French, a classmate, Aurelie, and I agreed to coach them. She and I soon realized, however, that this group was split between Hutu and Tutsi, their antagonism obvious through spiteful comments and the dark looks they exchanged.

Aurelie and I challenged the new girls to accept each other. Some seemed to take our advice, but others did not. Their prejudice was too deeply engrained.

In 1983 my parents moved to Bwegera, also in the Congo, where my father opened a small clinic. This town, on the road our family had traveled when I was seven, remained their home for more than a decade. I joined Papa and Mama there after my 1984 graduation. I was glad to support them in their many tasks, and I enjoyed getting reacquainted with my younger sisters and brothers.

A year later, Aunt Priscilla invited me to her wedding in Bugarama, in the southwest tip of Rwanda – in walking distance from both the Congo and Burundi borders. Accepting her invitation had life-changing consequences for me.

Priscilla's bridegroom, Alphonse, gave me a tour of Cimerwa, Rwanda's chief cement-processing company, for which he worked. As we walked, he explained that although Cimerwa belonged to the Rwandan state, Chinese specialists supervised the work, and some of the Rwandan engineers had trained in China. Jobs at this massive site ranged from quarrying raw materials and making cement to machine operation, construction, maintenance, landscaping, and office work.

Besides the cement factory, the vast complex included housing for six hundred employees, a school and nursery for their children, and a health center, to which six rooms and twelve beds were later added. There was even a resident doctor. I was impressed.

Later that year, I heard there was a job opening at Cimerwa. Determined to grab this chance, I returned to Bugarama.

There I found something better than a job. I found the man I was to marry.

5

Charles

PENDING MY HOPED-FOR JOB with Cimerwa, I stayed in Bugarama, in Alphonse and Priscilla's house. One evening some of their friends dropped in, so I prepared a meal of *ugari* with fish sauce. After dinner, over milky tea, everyone relaxed and talked.

One of the guests told me that twelve years previously, he had been studying toward the priesthood at Nyundo Catholic Seminary, near Gisenyi on Lake Kivu's northern shore. But when fellow Tutsi students were murdered in the 1973 wave of Hutu violence, he fled to the Congo and pursued a geology degree there instead. After graduating, he had returned to Rwanda and found a job with Cimerwa. He was in his thirties. His name was Charles.

I had no special interest in this young man, but he kept turning up at Priscilla's. One day he offered to show me where Cimerwa quarried travertine, a form of limestone, and I accepted his invitation.

It was obvious that Charles enjoyed walking; he also enjoyed explaining everything we passed. Pointing out a spring beside the path, he had me put my hands in its pool. To my surprise, the water was hot.

We became better acquainted as we walked. Charles said he came third in a family of eleven children. Actually there had been twelve, but one died in infancy. In 1959, his family had fled their home village of Mukoma – on a peninsula near the southern end of Lake Kivu – by boat to Idjwi Island. Refugee life had been harsh, so his childhood memories of the following months were unhappy ones. When the family returned to Rwanda, he and his siblings were slapped and punched by Hutu classmates in Mukoma's school.

Nyundo Catholic Seminary was one of the few places of higher education to accept Tutsi in Rwanda, so losing that opportunity, at age twenty, had been bitter for Charles. Even now, he told me, his presence at Cimerwa irked certain Hutu employees, who envied his university degree and his position in the company.

Charles said that all the discrimination and disappointment had made him disillusioned with religion; he was still Catholic, but only on paper. In contrast, my faith meant everything to me. I told him about my parents and family, my childhood, baptism, boarding school years – everything that had shaped my views. Although he could not comprehend my childlike faith, he said he respected it.

The more I saw Charles, the more I liked him. A peace-loving thinker, he was something of an introvert. He told me Cimerwa had shelves of science books, and he had read them all, because there was always more to learn. His direct manner, upright walk, and straightforward speech led me to trust him. He was strong and intelligent, of medium build, and sported a mustache. He was also constantly on guard, aware of the animosity of some of his colleagues.

Charles and I continued going for walks. One day, after watching the men and machines at work, he asked me into his office, in a building at the quarry site. Here he told me what was on his mind.

Charles said he enjoyed spending time with me, and he hoped we could be friends. In fact, he said, he hoped we might marry someday.

That was going too far for me. I was only twenty and had come to Bugarama in search of work. "What would my mother and father say," I asked, "if I turned up with a husband instead of a job?"

I became more reserved after this conversation. Love comes slowly. Rwanda was unfamiliar territory, and I felt far from home. I had always envisioned a marriage like my parents', so I was troubled that Charles lacked a sure belief. On the other hand, I hoped I might help restore him to faith . . . So I prayed, and I watched my admirer from a distance. Much later, Charles told me that he never gave up; he had believed I would someday say yes.

My first attempt to get work at Cimerwa failed, because an influential Hutu official – who resented Charles and knew of our friendship – forced me to leave Rwanda. As I crossed back into the Congo, he shook his fist. Several others joined him as he shouted insults behind me.

"You, Tutsi," he yelled, "you will never, never, never find work in Rwanda!"

I spent the next bleak months with an aunt in Burundi. Frustration over my failure to get my dream job – and over my humiliating ejection from Bugarama – smoldered into anger. Deciding I hated the place and all the interfering Hutu there, I refused to even listen to Rwandan news anymore. I found employment as an elementary school teacher and tried to start building a future in Burundi. But life seemed empty, and I cried a lot.

In December 1986, I decided to visit my family in the Congo. I was homesick; my birthday was approaching, and so was Christmas.

When I arrived in Bwegera, my parents had astonishing news: Charles had looked them up. They had liked him. My heart leapt. If Charles had made that effort to meet my father and mother, he was obviously still thinking seriously about me. Also, he had told them that the Hutu official who expelled me from Rwanda had moved away.

Gathering my courage, I returned to Bugarama in the first weeks of 1987. Priscilla and Alphonse welcomed me back into their home. Charles welcomed me, too. When Cimerwa's Chinese engineers threw a party, he brought me along, introducing me to everyone as his special friend.

Since I was eleven years younger than Charles, I felt shy around his fellow workers, who teased him about how young and beautiful I was. But when he and I were alone, I felt as comfortable as I did with my own brothers. Our friendship was spontaneous and natural, and we laughed a lot.

We resumed our walks, never forgetting to dip our hands into the hot spring. Once or twice a week, Charles took me out for grilled squash or banana. Sundays we often went for a drive in a Cimerwa car, occasionally making the ninety-minute trip to his childhood home. Here Charles introduced me to his parents, brothers, and sisters. Their compound was the largest in their village.

I loved Mukoma immediately and didn't mind its unpaved roads or its lack of electricity and running water. Children's voices, mingled with the lowing of cattle, made a fitting soundtrack for the pastoral scene of thatched huts scattered over grassy slopes, with Lake Kivu a shimmering backdrop.

If possible, it was even more beautiful at night. After the sun set over Congo's distant mountains, a chorus of frogs and insects tuned their evening concert, fireflies flickered across the hillsides, and the sky filled with stars. The first evening, I noticed twinkling lights filling the valley as well.

"Charles!" I exclaimed. "Is there a town down there?"

"No, Denise," he laughed. "You've forgotten Lake Kivu! That's the fishing fleet. Every boat has its lamp, to attract the fish."

Charles

As in my mother's home area, further north along Kivu's coast, most of Mukoma's population was Tutsi. The few Hutu families here were entwined with Tutsi through marriage. The prejudice Charles had experienced in elementary school seemed to have evaporated. Neighbors supported each other, and everyone made their living from agriculture, with fishing on the side. Children helped adults in the fields. Mukoma's red soil was fertile, yielding corn, sorghum, millet, beans, peanuts, onions, celery, and eggplant. Most families had sheep and goats as well as cows. Though not prosperous, theirs was a comfortable, harmonious existence.

As Charles and I walked or drove together, we discussed our hopes, dreams, strengths, and weaknesses. We became convinced that we were meant for each other, and we promised to stick together through good days and bad. After some months, he drove me to Kigali, Rwanda's capital, to get the working visa I needed in order to stay and work in Rwanda.

We set our wedding date for December 26, 1987.

Charles had planned for us to be married in the Catholic Church, in keeping with his background. But as soon as he appeared at my parents' home on Christmas Day, I knew something was wrong.

My levelheaded fiancé looked distraught. When I hurried to meet him, he said that the Hutu priest of Shangi Parish, to which Mukoma belonged, was refusing to marry us. The priest said it was because Charles was marrying a Protestant, yet he had known our intention for months and could have raised his objections before the last day.

"I bet it's because we're Tutsi," Charles said. We never learned the priest's reason, but he later went to prison for his part in the genocide against our people.

When Charles told my parents our predicament, they went straight to their own pastor. He assured us that everything would work out. After spending some hours talking with Charles, he baptized him. And the next day he married us.

Tateh Damaris, Tateh Ephraim, and many other relatives and friends from Rwanda and Burundi came to the Congo to attend our wedding. After the ceremony at my parents' church, we all drove to Rwanda to celebrate at my in-laws' compound in Mukoma. We had invited many more acquaintances to meet us there.

Frequently, Tutsi entering Rwanda from the Congo or Burundi would be refused entry; so I was apprehensive as our cortege approached the crossing into Rwanda – especially as some of our guests had no travel documents. Amazingly, none of us was detained. No one was even asked to display ID.

This was the same border at which I had been thrown out of Rwanda the previous year, so I felt like a queen when guards flung the barriers wide for my wedding party. This welcome seemed a Christmas wedding miracle, along with the sun that shone so brightly in usually wet December.

Mukoma villagers built a wedding canopy overlooking Lake Kivu, and my sisters-in-law cooked huge pots of rice over outdoor fires and prepared the traditional mixed grill of beef, lamb, and goat served with vegetables and onions. This was no small task. Since Charles and I both came from large families and had numerous friends, over four hundred wedding guests were pulling into Mukoma.

My bridegroom's coworkers arrived, including the Chinese engineers he knew so well. Even Cimerwa's three directors, who later became deadly enemies, joined our festivities that day. Everyone took part in the singing, and our guests drank as much banana beer and Fanta as they wished.

Blooming acacia and lemon trees and plantations of banana, avocado, coffee, and eucalyptus flowed down to the shore. There could be no lovelier setting for our wedding celebration, I was certain. The blue water sparkled below us, backed by Congo's green mountains fading into misty distance. Charles and I were perfectly happy.

Charles

Fortunately we had no inkling that our marriage would last only seven years – or that we would live together for less than three.

IN BUGARAMA, we were assigned a quality brick house in the row reserved for company management. Each spacious residence on our street was surrounded by tall cypress saplings and a high chain-link fence covered with rush matting for privacy.

Settling in and decorating our home was a pleasure for us both – especially for me. I felt like a bird adding the final feathers to its nest.

With free medical service on site, plus a nursery school financed by the business, almost everything we might need was at hand. Nyakabuye, the market town where we bought fresh vegetables and fruit on Saturdays, was a mile and a half from Bugarama's factory and housing complex. The company kept the road in excellent condition.

High-ranking staff, including my husband, used Cimerwa cars for trips; a white bus – nicknamed "Apartheid" by those who were not allowed to use it – took wives of executive employees to Muganza every Friday for shopping. I was one of these privileged few. When common workers needed to travel, they had to catch a ride on the Daihatsu Transporter that carried both goods and passengers.

Walking was still our favorite way to relax. Evenings after work, we often hiked out to our vegetable plot, where we planted some basic crops. We were entitled to this allotment, near the quarry where Charles had first proposed to me, because of his company status.

Or we strolled around the factory grounds. We would visit the night crew, and Charles had them show me their work. Most impressive was the kiln where a mixture of red clay, quartz, travertine, and slurry was heated to 2,700 degrees Fahrenheit – approximately the temperature of molten lava. We had to wear special glasses to look into this furnace, even though we kept a safe distance from the heat.

A week into married life, I started working for Cimerwa, in administration. I purchased supplies, maintained office equipment, and was responsible for tickets to the workers' canteen. I liked my supervisor, a Chinese lady called Li.

Another young employee, Annemarie, came by each day for the meal tickets. She took time to help me build my Kinyarwanda vocabulary and improve my pronunciation, and we became friends. We soon found we had much in common. Like me, Annemarie sought God's guidance in every aspect of life, and we shared our hope that our husbands would someday do the same.

Before entering marriage, I had pictured it as heaven on earth. Now I realized that not every problem disappears at your wedding. In fact, new ones emerge.

Beginning and ending each day with prayer had always been essential for me. After Charles and I were married, I expected my husband to lead ours, as my father had always done for my family.

Looking blank, he said, "I have no idea how to pray."

Startled, I reminded him that he had been baptized before our wedding.

"My last prayer was at seminary, when the Hutu were trying to kill us," he admitted.

"Just offer a word of thanks, from your heart," I said. As Charles did, I mentally added, "Help me win him for you."

Church had also been central in my life, so I was distressed that Charles spent Sundays on other activities. I joined his jaunts to visit friends, playing the loyal wife, but I missed spiritual fellowship.

One day I opened the door in answer to a knock and was surprised to see five people outside. I recognized them as Cimerwa colleagues, and they now introduced themselves as a prayer group. I invited them in.

The leader's name was Oscar. He said his wife, Consolée, had heard that a young believer had moved in, and they wanted to get acquainted. I told them my situation, and we were soon reading the Bible and singing together. Oscar and Consolée soon became some of my closest friends, and through them I got to know more Christians in the area.

CHARLES AND I were both thrilled, a year into our marriage, to realize I was pregnant. Coming from big families, we both wanted the same.

Secretly hoping our first child would be a boy and our second a girl, as in my own family, I dreamed of raising sons and daughters in the fear of God. My husband's dream was not identical to mine, yet he, too, meant to do his utmost for our child. He was keen to provide a good education and to raise a well-behaved family. Respectful children give their parents a good reputation in our culture.

As the weeks and months inched toward my due date, I seesawed between expectation and anxiety. I missed my mother. "Lord, I don't know how to raise a child," I prayed. "You will have to show me how. And please, protect our little one." I was determined to make our home a warm, nurturing place where our baby should lack nothing. Meanwhile, I kept regular appointments with my doctor, exercised, and read books for expectant mothers.

Charles and I took a day off work to go shopping in Bukavu. Our spree was well worth the twenty-five-mile drive and the border crossing into the Congo. Exploring the modern stores, comparing prices, and finally making our choices thrilled me with anticipation. We could barely fit our purchases into the Cimerwa car. Our bassinet and blankets were the best available, and I sorted the baby clothes several times during our return drive, trying to decide which were cutest. Even their smell excited me.

I went into labor on the first of August. Charles called Oscar and Consolée, and the four of us drove to Mibilizi Hospital together, in a Cimerwa car. Early the next morning, August 2, 1989, our baby arrived.

My husband took our firstborn son into his arms. "You did it!" he said, looking from me to the baby, and back again. "You wonderful woman!" He kissed us both.

I was deeply content. Our child was safely here. We were a complete family.

Charles gave me *igikoma cy'umubyeyi*. Every new Rwandan mother enjoys this healthy drink, made from milk and sorghum, that betokens future wellbeing. Friends, relatives, and colleagues came to congratulate us and admire the baby. Charles and I named him Rukundo Charles-Vital. Rukundo means love, and Vital was the name of my husband's best friend.

NINE MONTHS LATER, in May 1990, my husband traveled to Bujumbura, the capital of Burundi, on Cimerwa's behalf. Since my brother Phocas lived there, Charles decided to drop in on him. And since it happened to be Sunday, Charles waited outside the church. There, from the doorway, he listened to the sermon.

As usual, I watched for my husband's return. He would always park the car at Cimerwa and walk the short distance to our home. This time, I noticed a spring in his step and a sparkle in his eyes. "Denise, I'm a born-again Christian!" he called as he approached.

When he had heard the preacher's words, "The blood of Jesus has power to wash the dirt from our lives," Charles told me, all his past sins had appeared before him. Admitting he had been baptized before our wedding primarily for my sake, he now sincerely dedicated his life to Christ. "Denise, I will pray with you from now on," he said. "Jesus says he gives living water. With you, I will keep going to him for that water, so I'm not pulled back into my old ways."

Charles

A week after his trip, as Charles and I walked hand in hand to the service in Mashesha, I overheard a neighbor say, "What? Educated people believe in Jesus?" I didn't care what the neighbors thought. I had received my heart's desire, and I sensed that our family now had a firm foundation.

Formerly, Charles had disparaged Hutu behind their backs at every opportunity. I never heard such talk from him again. Instead, I heard a lot more laughter – until they took him away.

6

Trouble

ON OCTOBER 1, 1990, an electric current pulsed through the land when radios announced that the Rwandan Patriotic Front had invaded from Uganda. The RPF was comprised mainly of Tutsi exiles and refugees who had fled Hutu violence in Rwanda in earlier decades. Successive governments had persecuted them in Uganda, yet they were arbitrarily denied reentry to Rwanda, year after year.

In a renewed attempt to return, the RPF invaded Rwanda this first of October, but the Hutu government, supported by French military aid, rebuffed them. Government leaders labeled them *inyangarwanda*, "people who hate Rwanda," and *inyenzi*, "cockroaches."

Three days later, radio broadcasts reported that the RPF had attacked the capital city, Kigali. This was fake news; Habyarimana's forces had in fact stopped the invasion at the Uganda border. Cleverly contriving a link between the RPF and the Tutsi minority in Rwanda, the government spread the word that "*inyenzi* have infiltrated everywhere."

Their fearmongering led to arrests throughout the country. Who would be next? With the tension building, Charles and I decided to fast and pray on Saturday, October 6. At two o'clock that afternoon, we were kneeling in our bedroom when the door flew open and two policemen burst in. They grabbed Charles, who gave me a desperate look as they hustled him away to their car and drove off.

Sick and hopeless, I lay down on our bed and wept. That evening I vomited, the beginning of stomach problems that plagued me for the next fourteen years.

That night, one of my husband's colleagues phoned, urging me to flee the country. He had heard a rumor that the rebels – as Hutu called the RPF – were now attacking from nearby Burundi as well as from Uganda, implying worse troubles ahead. But what could I do? I could not simply take my one-year-old and disappear without knowing what was happening to Charles – or even where he was.

A commotion roused me at five o'clock the next morning. Peeking between the curtains, I saw two military trucks packed with soldiers, as well as several soldiers standing in the road with two-way radios. These were saying that Bugarama had been infiltrated by RPF – another false report.

"Where are *inyenzi*?" one shouted through a bullhorn as they moved slowly down the street.

During this Sunday morning, a company colleague came by for my husband's office keys. He did not know where Charles was, but he offered to help me search. We first walked to Muganza to inquire at the local jail, but Charles was not there. Then we drove to the patrol offices at the Burundi and Congo borders; here too no one knew anything. I realized then that Charles had to be at the central prison in Cyangugu. Back at home, I could not concentrate. For my toddler's sake, however, I fought my fears and tried to keep calm.

After the weekend, I learned that Charles was not the only Cimerwa employee to have been apprehended. At least six other prominent Tutsi had been arrested in the factory town.

That Monday, all Tutsi homes in Bugarama were searched for weapons. I hoped that since Charles had already been detained, our house would be bypassed. But a police car pulled up at my gate, and Bugarama's mayor got out with a police officer and Sebatware, one of Cimerwa's three directors. Entering, they told me my husband was being charged with sabotage. Since Charles was responsible for Cimerwa's explosives, he was particularly suspect, they said – and they had come to search my house.

I opened the doors to all our rooms and cupboards, showing we had nothing to hide. The men confiscated several photos, plus the receipt for a used Land Rover Charles had bought. Before leaving, they arrested Dominique, a Hutu teenager who helped with chores around the house. They kept him in jail two weeks, trying to make him say that Charles had exchanged the Land Rover for dynamite. Dominique was beaten, but he never denounced my husband.

From the day of the search, Cimerwa directors posted a guard at my gate. Alphonse dropped by one morning to ask how I was coping. He was arrested as soon as he left my house and was jailed for two weeks. After that, people stopped coming to see me.

In a matter of days, my neighbors had become hostile. At work, almost no one talked to me. I had never felt so isolated. The whole town seemed permeated with suspicion. Bonafrida, a Tutsi nurse in Cimerwa's clinic, told me that Hutu patients no longer trusted her to give them injections.

On Sunday evening, October 14, my phone rang. It was Sebatware. In his abrupt manner, he said that prosecutors in Cyangugu wanted to interrogate me. "Be ready in five minutes!" he ordered.

My mind went into a spin. What did they want? As I hastily pulled on some slacks beneath my *kitenge*, I tried to think what was best for Charles-Vital. Should I leave him with neighbors? But I might not come back . . . I decided to take him along.

As I lifted my sleeping one-year-old from his crib, the company vehicle pulled up outside. Throughout the thirty-five-mile trip, I battled anxiety: What were they doing to Charles? What would happen to our child? What would happen to me?

In Cyangugu, three prosecutors grilled me about friends, relatives, acquaintances – in this province, in the cement plant, and abroad. They quizzed me about people in the snapshots the mayor had confiscated, which magazines my father-in-law read, where my family was. . . . I answered all their questions. I had nothing to hide.

Before letting me go, they warned me to tell no one of this interrogation. If I did, they would be sure to learn of it, they said, and there would be "consequences." Then they dismissed me. But I had no sense of relief as Charles-Vital and I were driven home through the dark, nor any feeling of security as I carried him into our empty house.

Toward the end of October, I went to the mayor's office, requesting to visit my husband in prison. The mayor replied that I was not a Rwandan citizen and therefore had no rights in this country. Reminding him of my official permission to live and work in Rwanda, I again pleaded to visit Charles.

"No!" he yelled. "Get out of here!"

And this was the man who used to shoot hoops with Charles on Cimerwa's basketball court, stopping by our house afterward to shower. . . .

Defeated, I stood in the road outside the mayor's office. Looking upward, I silently cried out, reminding Jesus how he had fled Bethlehem with his parents, though neither he nor they had done any wrong – this was how it felt being Tutsi in Rwanda.

Cement trucks drove past, coating me with dust. I remained rooted to the spot. A driver rolled down his window, offering a lift, but I dumbly shook my head.

Finally, I walked home and wept. Then I turned to the Bible. In the third chapter of Ezekiel, I read, "But I will make you as unyielding and hardened as they are. I will make your forehead like the hardest stone, harder than flint." These words emboldened me to try again.

This time I approached Sebatware. Although I knew his callous character, I walked into the director's office, putting my trust in God.

"You are not Rwandan!" Sebatware challenged when I entered. "Why did your parents leave this country?" He knew they had fled for political reasons, so I ignored his question, telling him instead that I wanted to visit Charles in Cyangugu Prison. His grim expression never softened, but he handed me a pass, granting freedom of movement on the company's behalf. He also gave me use of a company car and driver.

Since I had the pass and the vehicle, I invited Oscar and Bonafrida to join me. Bonafrida's husband, Silas, had been arrested, as had Consolée, Oscar's wife. Consolée was pregnant at the time. She was later released to the hospital for the birth of their daughter, Ruth, but was then returned to prison.

We three made the trip to Cyangugu on Thursday, November 1. The road was so crowded with some kind of demonstration that our driver had to stop the car. The marchers were carrying tree trunks and shouting slogans. When we were able to make out their words, we realized this was a Hutu victory march celebrating the death, some weeks previous, of RPF leader Fred Rwigema. Carrying logs represented taking him to be buried. They were threatening to do the same to whoever might replace Rwigema; I heard Paul Kagame's name, purposely mispronounced *Kagome*, meaning "bad man."

Little did these demonstrators dream that Paul Kagame would not only lead the RPF to victory over their regime in less than four years, he would become Rwanda's president for more than twenty.

We passed several checkpoints on the way to Cyangugu, but our car was always waved through, thanks to its Cimerwa logo. Everyone knew Cimerwa was run by extremist Hutu.

Seeing Charles was a shock. His head was shaved. In less than a month he had lost weight, his face had become haggard, and his skin had taken a strange whitish pallor. He was still wearing the denim jacket and jeans in which he had been arrested.

To encourage him, I described our little son's latest achievements. Then I gave him a Bible and passed on my parents' greeting, Isaiah 41:10, "So do not fear, for I am with you; do not be dismayed, for I am your God. I will strengthen you and help you, I will uphold you with my righteous right hand."

Other than that, we could say little. Prison guards were writing down every sentence. We could only look at each other, letting our eyes say what words could not. Reluctantly I took leave of my husband, trying not to communicate my loneliness, which would only have increased his own.

On Friday morning, I returned the pass to Sebatware, who tore it up. He then summoned all Cimerwa employees to gather on the concrete outside the company health center. When everyone was assembled and silent, Sebatware announced that from now on, no loitering or discussion would be tolerated on the factory premises.

"Trust is a thing of the past!" he said, glowering around at the six hundred faces.

Bonafrida and I did not let this announcement deter us. We depended on conversation to buoy our spirits, since both our husbands were in prison, and we continued to speak whenever we met.

The next time Oscar and I visited our spouses, I asked a guard why certain Cimerwa Tutsi employees had been arrested. He told me to ask my boss. Oscar and I decided to approach the three top Cimerwa officials: Sebatware, the general director; Gasasira, the

commercial director; and Casimir, the technical director. Bonafrida came with us.

We asked these three directors to intervene on behalf of our
family members in prison. They replied that they could do nothing,
claiming they were not responsible for the arrests. Bonafrida flared
up at this, accusing Casimir of wanting her husband's job for his
brother-in-law. The directors promptly fired her and forced her to
move back to eastern Rwanda with her two children, although
her husband remained in prison in the southwest. Casimir's
brother-in-law was indeed given Silas's job. I missed Bonafrida. I
never saw her again.

By now it was December 1990, and the "Hutu Ten Commandments" had been published by *Kangura*, a widely read pro-regime
magazine. Among its commandments, the document stated that
the armed forces must consist exclusively of Hutu, that any Hutu
man marrying a Tutsi was a traitor, and that no Hutu should
employ Tutsi or even feel compassion toward them.

Annemarie was one of the only people I could still relate to at
work; the others found ways to show their spite. A young colleague
took away my office chair, telling me Tutsi had no right to sit
anymore. Thankfully, the Chinese supervisor intervened and made
him return my chair.

During this lonely period, I started keeping a journal. After my
child was tucked into bed at night I found a measure of comfort
in jotting down my fears and frustrations, my prayers, or any
thoughts that stirred me while reading the Bible. Entries were
random, because I would open to any page, date it, and start to
write. I didn't care that it was not chronological – the little book
was for me alone to read, and I treasured it. I kept it hidden in a
cupboard, where no one could probe its contents.

How I appreciated my little son's companionship, although I
worried about what the future held for him. He was a late talker,

but he found other ways to communicate. He would toddle around me as I sat in the backyard, bringing me pebbles or taking my hand to show me something. In the evenings, I often held him on my lap and sang to him from my hymnal. He would "sing" along, making sounds – without words – on perfect pitch. I was astonished when he turned the pages to his favorite song. How did he recognize it?

In March 1991, Rwanda's political climate improved somewhat. The wider world had noted that Tutsi were disappearing, and the Hutu government had to tread more carefully if it wanted a good international image.

I observed this shift when a lawyer came to investigate the arrests of Tutsi Cimerwa employees. Annemarie slid a sheet of carbon paper onto his clipboard, beneath his note-taking. Thus she and I learned that one of our supervisors – who was later responsible for many murders – made no claims against Charles or the other imprisoned Tutsi at this time.

I noticed, too, that people were no longer afraid to visit me at home. I welcomed the change in our community and at work, but, in hindsight, it gave me a false sense of safety. I was lulled into thinking life could return to normal.

After one of Annemarie's frequent evening visits, I accompanied her to my front gate. Charles-Vital, as usual, was at my side, clinging to my hand. A man was stumbling down the road, obviously drunk. He veered in our direction, his eyes on my son.

Glancing at his wrist, as if checking the time, he said, "Hey, little guy! I come from Cyangugu. I just signed your father's release papers."

Then he turned to continue his zigzag course. Annemarie and I looked at each other, eyebrows raised at this bizarre encounter; neither of us had ever seen the man before. A few days later, on March 26, Charles was inexplicably released, after nearly six months in prison.

The evening of my husband's homecoming, several friends came to our house, bringing food and drink for an impromptu party. Engrossed in conversation with one of them, Charles did not at first notice Charles-Vital banging his leg and singing, over and over, *"Papa, Papa, Imana ishimwe cyane,"* "Papa, Papa, give great praise to God!" – changing the words of a hymn to fit the occasion. Our child had never enunciated these words before.

Charles lifted him in a heartfelt hug. My heart was singing too as I watched them; we were a complete family. I hoped that our troubles were over – that now we could live happily ever after, as in my mother's legends. We would serve the Lord together, leading the life I had envisioned at our wedding.

Despite our relief and pleasure, however, Charles seemed somewhat guarded. He shared few details of what he had endured in prison, beyond saying that he had been beaten. I did not press. I was sure he would tell me more once he had recovered – never guessing how brief our reunion would be.

In November, Cimerwa's three directors told Charles he was fired. Perhaps with him out of the way, those responsible for his arrest could avoid embarrassment – or one of the colleagues who had always envied his position could replace him.

We were dismayed, of course, but we were also afraid. We knew from experience that anyone in the directors' bad books was in danger. Charles decided it would be best for him to disappear in Kigali and live incognito there. I was heartsick. Kigali was 185 miles away. It was also the center of growing conflict, as emerging political factions were violently sparring. Even lack of political interest could be fatal there these days. Cars had been lured into traps and burned, with their passengers. Nonetheless, Charles departed.

But what about me and our little son? I applied for a transfer to Cimerwa's Kigali branch, but the directors were quick to remind me that my working visa covered only my job in Bugarama. If I left, it would become invalid. Theobald, a new company official responsible for worker welfare, told me I was lucky to be in the relative safety of Bugarama. He had just come from Kigali. So I had no choice but to accept this further separation.

Charles visited as often as he could, arriving after dark and leaving before sunrise. To prevent neighbors noticing and alerting his rivals, he covered many miles on foot before catching a bus to the capital. My cousin Manasseh, who also worked for Cimerwa in Bugarama, often accompanied Charles on these predawn hikes to the distant bus terminal.

A few days after firing my husband, Cimerwa's directors issued me an ultimatum to vacate our house. As an executive employee, Charles had been entitled to it; as a common worker, I was not.

I loved this home that Charles and I had shared. Thanks to his good salary, I had been able to decorate it with beautiful traditional handicrafts and wall hangings. My costly Burundian chinaware, purchased for our wedding, made a handsome display. We had quality furniture. My clothing, too, was of the best material; when my colleague Li returned to China, she had sold me her extra clothes and shoes – all designer products.

I had enjoyed living in style. Now I would have to step down. I felt insulted. Hadn't I always done my utmost for the business? And my husband had been their best geologist – where would Cimerwa be without his expertise? And why would the directors evict a mother alone, I stormed. But I knew the answer: a Tutsi woman was not meant to prosper. Humiliated, I started to pack.

Charles-Vital and I moved into an apartment in a sturdy brick duplex. Theobald arranged this move for me. Though smaller than our previous home, this building had the same strong front gate and high surrounding fence.

Our half included a living room, four bedrooms, a bathroom, and a storeroom. There was also a small room for our live-in help. Our backyard held the kitchen hut that goes with every Rwandan home; we would not want an indoor kitchen because we cook with wood and prefer to keep the smoke outdoors. Beyond this yard was a large compound where all Cimerwa's Chinese employees lived. Their spacious, fenced-off grounds and banana grove were protected by security guards and dogs.

Few sounds penetrated the wall separating my apartment from the other half of our house. I barely knew the Hutu couple living there, although we would greet each other in passing. They were known by the name "Kibuye," because they had come from that area – not the Kibuye in Burundi, where I was born, but a Rwandan region of the same name.

I had far more contact with my friend Goretti and her husband Viateur in the next house. They were Tutsi and attended a nearby Catholic church. Their three children, Fiston, Kim, and Diane, were much older than my little son, but they enjoyed playing with him. And if Charles-Vital got sick, Goretti popped in to visit. In fact, they seemed like family.

Goretti and Viateur's apartment was identical to mine. The other half of their duplex was occupied by a Hutu couple belonging to my church. The husband, Marcel, was a physician's assistant who ran Cimerwa's medical facility.

In front of my new home, our side street opened onto the main road, across which was the cement plant's main entrance, clearly visible from my bedroom window. Casimir's Musikiti Bar beside this gate was a popular place for employees to stop for a beer after work. Casimir had clout as Cimerwa's technical director, and he had not overlooked this opportunity to make money on the side. Evenings got rowdy at the bar, and it took me several weeks to get used to the noise – especially on Saturday nights.

One day, after I was settled into my new home, a Hutu neighbor came to visit. "Last night I dreamed I was in a cemetery with fresh graves everywhere," she said. "Many people had been buried within a short time. Then I noticed you, Denise, standing in one of those graves! I was astonished to see you alive, and I called to others, who went to fetch your husband. They returned with a man. But he was a stranger."

I recorded her dream in my journal, but to God I prayed: "If this weird message is from you, what is it supposed to mean? Why can't you give me the hope I hunger for?"

Another Hutu colleague, Vianney, came to see me in April 1992, saying, "God has this message for you, Denise: 'What no human being can do for you, I, the Lord will do for you. You will have many difficulties, but I will protect and bless you.'"

I wrote down Vianney's words as well; but again, they were small comfort. I didn't want "many difficulties." I wanted God's reassurance that everything would be all right – that our land would have peace and that Charles would come home.

7
Tightening Net

AT 7:30 IN THE MORNING on October 5, 1992, our second
son was born. My husband's sister Mary and her friend Naomi
came from Mukoma to help. I appreciated their excellent care.
Still, I ached for Charles. I missed his support during my labor, and
after it was safely accomplished I yearned to see his shining eyes,
feel his admiring kiss, hear his jubilant laugh and approving words.

I also longed for him to help name our child, a decision we make
only after a baby is born, in our culture. In my husband's absence,
I named our son Mugisha Christian. I chose Mugisha, meaning
blessing, because of God's promise to bless me in spite of difficulties, and Christian because Jesus Christ was our only hope.

Around this time, the government's Ministry of Mining and
Industry assigned Charles a new job in Kamembe. Now less than
thirty miles from home, he could visit more often, though he still
came and went only in the dark.

Sometimes he took three-year-old Charles-Vital back with him
for a few days. Kamembe is not far from Mukoma, and Charles-Vital

loved meeting his grandparents, exploring his father's childhood village, and swimming with him in Lake Kivu. My son clings to these memories. They are all he has of his father.

Many Rwandans were displaying political flags outside their homes in those days. Charles-Vital asked me what the emblems meant, and I tried to explain in simple terms a young child could understand. "We need a flag," he responded eagerly. "We belong to Jesus' party!" Taping a sheet of white paper to a stick, he planted it at our gate.

When Christian was ten days old, I noticed a bruise-like swelling on his head. Concerned, I showed Mary, who agreed that we should get medical advice. As I had no vehicle, we decided to walk the mile or so to Mashesha Health Center, up a hill across the Njambwe River. I carried my handbag and an umbrella for protection from the sun. Mary followed, my baby tied onto her back in his *ingobyi*.

Nearing the river, we were alarmed to see a roadblock at the center of the bridge. To circumvent this crossing would have meant a long detour, so we cautiously approached. A makeshift sign proclaimed this barrier the property of MRND, an extremist Hutu party.

The guards looked terrifying. Huge banana leaves, tied to their heads, covered their upper bodies. Their faces were disguised with mud. I had heard that members of opposing political factions – or anyone not belonging to their own – could be refused passage, beaten, or worse at such checkpoints.

As we stepped hesitantly onto the bridge, one of the sinister figures moved out to bar the way. Reaching toward me, he demanded, "Your party affiliation card."

Sensing our peril, I passed him Christian's birth certificate, verifying that my child had been born in Mashesha Health Center earlier that month. The young man studied it from beneath his banana leaf, then slid his glare to the infant on Mary's back. I held my breath as the mud-ringed eyes flicked back to my face. Turning abruptly to his comrades, he barked, "Let them go!"

At the clinic a medical assistant, Karekezi, examined Christian. He said the hematoma was not serious and offered to treat it immediately. After the small incision was sutured and dressed, we were allowed to take him home.

Mary and I were only too aware of the hazards of our return trek, but there was no question of staying at the health center or taking the long detour. Danger could lurk on any route we chose, and it was already afternoon. I needed to get back to Charles-Vital, who had spent the day with my teenage helper.

Uneasily, Mary and I walked down the hill. Even before reaching the river, we encountered a new roadblock. Again menacing guards confronted passersby; but these belonged to a different political party, MDR. They glanced at us suspiciously, then let us through, telling us to be quick. Their attention was focused across the Njambwe.

The MRND had shifted their barricade to the Bugarama side of the river, so the bridge now lay between the two. As we hastened across, I was shocked to recognize young men from my neighborhood at the MRND checkpoint. At least their leader, Yussuf Munyakazi, was not among them this time.

My husband and I had known Yussuf as a genial, easygoing guy. A rich farmer and businessman, he owned most of the rice fields surrounding Bugarama and kept close ties with Cimerwa's directors. Back in 1989, Charles and I traveled with him, in a Cimerwa car, to the wedding of a colleague. Throughout that drive, we had talked and joked, Yussuf even teaching us a Muslim song to perform at the party. A couple years later, however, Charles and I noticed a change. Yussuf had become arrogant, his tone contemptuous. We wondered what had happened.

Much later, I learned that in 1991 Yussuf was invited, with other MRND leaders, to a secret meeting with President

Habyarimana – the meeting in which the "final solution of the Tutsi problem" was planned. From that day, Yussuf Munyakazi had been covertly training Hutu youth for genocide. Of course, I knew none of this as Mary and I made our way warily over the bridge toward Yussuf's recruits.

Like their rivals across the river, the MRND ordered Mary and me to hurry on. Both factions clearly wanted to get at each other. We were only yards past the scene when their verbal sparring resumed, the clamor of their yells propelling us on our way. Then we heard shots.

When we reached home, shaken but unharmed, the neighbor's houseboy met us, howling with mirth. "You should have heard your kid, when I asked him what party your family belongs to," he hooted.

My own helper interrupted indignantly. "You didn't *ask* Charles-Vital," he challenged hotly. "You *told* him to say his family belongs to Inkotanyi!"

"Well, OK," the first conceded with a shrug, "but you should have heard the kid's answer: 'No, we don't belong to Inkotanyi. We belong to Jesus' party!'"

Mimicking the childish words once more, the Hutu houseboy turned to go, still chortling.

This was no laughing matter. I was appalled that this teenager had tried to trap me through my innocent three-year-old. He knew as well as I did that anyone connected with Inkotanyi, the party associated with RPF, was fair game for imprisonment or death. There was danger when I ventured out, and danger when I returned to my own street.

Oh Charles, please come home! If only you knew how much I am struggling here . . .

A YEAR LATER, in October 1993, Burundi's Hutu president, Ndadaye, was assassinated by Tutsi members of his own military.

This coup triggered further violence in that country: Tutsi killing Hutu and Hutu killing Tutsi.

Since Bugarama is less than five miles from the Burundi border, the tension in our community was such that no Tutsi could even go shopping.

Militant Hutu placed checkpoints on every road through our region. These differed from earlier barriers erected by opposing factions – this time they all had a common enemy: the Tutsi. Even footpaths were under surveillance.

By this time, I knew I was carrying our third child, which only intensified my fear. Feeling besieged by danger, I prayed often with Oscar and Consolée.

The political situation became dreadfully personal one day. A Tutsi friend of mine had married a Hutu policeman; now she was found dead, her throat cut. My informant, a work colleague, went on to say that, according to rumor, her own husband had betrayed her.

My shock was so intense, I felt pain in my chest. Never had someone this close to me been killed.

Dear God, have mercy! And please, let me never feel such terror again.

My stomach problems worsened. I felt ill whenever I thought of my murdered friend.

CHARLES SLIPPED into the house for one of his rare visits on the evening of January 23, 1994. He had become adept at skirting roadblocks by night.

After treasuring some time with our little boys and tucking them into bed, we heard a knock at the door – a sound that froze my heart these days. Charles checked through a side window before unlocking and opening the door.

It was Felix, a man from a neighboring village. He told us God had sent him with a message: We two must make sure there was peace between us, forgiving one another and resolving any misunderstandings or grudges while there was still time. That's all he said. Then he was gone.

Our eyes met. I was first to speak.

"Yes, Charles, he's right. I have not fully trusted you. I noticed that ever since your release from prison, you always kept your passport in your pocket. I was afraid you intended to leave the country without me and the children. Please forgive me!"

"Oh, Denise," he responded, "I had no such plan. I kept my passport on me because I never knew when I might be stopped and questioned. But I'm the one who needs your forgiveness. At work, my colleagues keep kidding around, telling me you are seeing other men. I've always defended you – but their words planted doubt in my heart. I'm so sorry!"

We both had tears in our eyes as we reaffirmed our loyalty and then prayed together. Life had never seemed so precious. Our lively sons were growing, our baby was due in less than three months, and we were more deeply in love than ever.

We spent most of the night talking. I told him how, with all the murders and checkpoints, it felt like a net was tightening around us. Charles spoke of his difficult earlier years: fleeing for his life and struggling as a refugee, first as a child and later as a college student. He hoped our children's childhood and youth could be more secure and peaceful than his. I promised to do my best for them.

Before sunrise, Charles slipped away.

Felix was not the only one who sensed that time was running out. An old woman, Ngelina, visited me regularly. She said God had sent her to encourage me and to pray for my children, particularly for my unborn child. I appreciated her concern – but fortunately, I had no premonition of how my third child would be born.

EASTER CAME on April third that year. Charles managed to come home for the occasion, arriving late Friday night – Good Friday, crucifixion day. There was no question of leaving the house to attend Easter services. It would have been far too dangerous for my husband to be seen here; even I was afraid to go outside. Our family spent the holiday indoors, and the time together passed too quickly.

Sometime during the night between Monday and Tuesday, Charles told me it was time for him to go. At the thought of him leaving, I started to cry and couldn't stop.

"Denise, what's wrong?" he asked.

I did not try to answer. How could I explain that sorrow, heavy as a house, was pressing me down? How could I share my foreboding that this was our final farewell?

Placing his hands on my shoulders and looking into my eyes, Charles said, "Have peace!" Those were his last words to me.

Then he walked out our bedroom door. I followed to the gate, not wanting to let him go, holding in my sobs for fear of the neighbors. His arms went around me and our unborn child again, but he said nothing further. What could he have said?

He kissed me once more, then vanished into the darkness.

MY HUSBAND'S PREDAWN DEPARTURE was on Tuesday, April 5. The next day, Wednesday evening, President Habyarimana's plane was shot down. And Thursday morning, just after six o'clock, Goretti gave me the news at the fence between our backyards. We didn't know it yet, but the genocide against the Tutsi had begun.

That Thursday night there was a sharp rap at the gate. It was a distant relative, Joram, who also lived and worked in Bugarama. He kept glancing behind him and spoke fast as he explained that a Hutu friend, Ezekias, was helping him and his wife escape to the Congo – and he had come now to ask if I wanted to go along.

Ezekias had told Joram of Tutsi being killed after they sought refuge in a church. During past conflicts, no one had shed blood in churches, which were considered holy ground and safe sanctuary. I later learned that at one church in Hanika, not far from where my mother's extended family lived, around ten thousand Tutsi had sought refuge. Interahamwe surrounded them and threw grenades into the church, pursuing and cutting down any Tutsi who fled. Most of my mother's family was wiped out that day.

Not allowing my imagination to run amok, I thanked Joram. But I told him that in my condition, and with my dependents, I was in no state to flee. He disappeared into the dark, and I relocked the gate.

In the following days, our household settled into an uneasy routine. Formerly the factory had generated a steady background din, twenty-four hours a day, six days a week. Now its silence magnified the suspense shrouding our town. I'm sure my children felt it. Their play in our apartment, or in the backyard when the April rain abated, lacked its usual zest. Each evening, I gathered everyone in the living room for prayer.

One morning during this stressful week, I came upon a worksheet Charles-Vital had brought home from Sunday school a month earlier. It was a drawing of two people, one leaning on a cane and the other assisting. Its caption read, "God comforts his people in their sorrow."

Showing my cousin, I said, "Look, Manasseh, this page is a sign – it's God's promise to take care of us!"

"No, Denise," he replied dully, shaking his head. "The time has come for all Tutsi to die."

It was terrible to hear such despairing words from my cousin. He was twenty-nine, like me, and was engaged to be married. Just a week or two before, I had heard him and his fiancée, Valerie, discussing wedding plans.

A few nights after Anselm and Manasseh's arrival at my place, another colleague, Lambert, slipped furtively by, asking if his wife, Francine, could move in as well, with their young child and two-week-old baby. Lambert had just learned that his name was on the death list, he said, and he wanted his family out of harm's way.

I knew this couple well. I told Lambert, however, that I did not think it wise for his wife and children to join me. My apartment, already crowded, was as likely as any to be attacked. My heart was heavy as he turned away.

On Wednesday morning, April 13, Goretti told me Cimerwa's directors had just instructed her husband, Viateur, with other company mechanics, to drive the Chinese workers across the border into Burundi. All foreign nationals were being evacuated from Rwanda, she said.

From my back window, I watched our forty-three Chinese colleagues hastening from their compound to the waiting vehicles, their suitcases bumping behind them. Their faces were set, and they did not call out in farewell to their old neighbors. Most did not even look back.

Doors slammed, engines roared to life, and then they were gone.

8

April 16

CIMERWA IS A MASSIVE BUSINESS to this day. The company produces 600,000 tons of cement per year, supplying all of Rwanda and exporting to other African nations as well. Its Bugarama plant is still the biggest employer in the region.

Viewers checking the website's timeline will notice something odd, however. Among various years' achievements, the 1994 entry reads, "Operations suspended during genocide which saw 58 Cimerwa team members lose their lives." It does not state how many of those fifty-eight lost their lives at the hands of other Cimerwa team members. I knew a number of the victims – and their killers.

In all, 342 Tutsi were murdered in Bugarama during the genocide. But numbers never tell the whole story; they can't convey that each of these people was a unique individual with loves and hurts, sorrows and joys, disappointments and yearnings. Some had lived long years; some were babies. Some died quickly; others were tortured.

The killing reached Bugarama on April 16. How gladly I would forget all I saw that day, but – as war veterans can confirm – such images are seared into the brain as if by a camera's flash.

Why revisit that day's events, then, if they were so horrific? I feel I owe it to the people who died; if I don't tell, who will even know that they lived? Also, I write for the sake of history. If a nation's shameful deeds are not to be repeated, they must be recognized and remembered – not swept under the rug. As harsh as it is, American youth need to learn how Native American peoples were exterminated; Germans have to know what their country did to the Jews; and Turks must acknowledge the Armenian genocide. Mass evil can break out at any place where that one group despises another. In Bosnia, people who had previously lived peaceably as neighbors carried out the 1995 massacre of Muslims at Srebrenica. And in 2017, ethnic cleansing in Myanmar claimed around ten thousand Rohingya lives.

So, as a witness to the genocide against the Tutsi, I must tell what happened, no matter how painful it is for me to write. I hope my account will help ensure that nothing like this ever happens again, anywhere on earth. But I also write because genocide is not the end of the story – not for me and not for my beloved country.

IT IS STILL HARD for me to believe that the sun rose as usual on April 16, but in fact it was a beautiful Saturday morning. Since the factory was silent, I could hear birds singing. The sky had cleared again, with no sign of rain.

If it hadn't been for the dread weighing me down, this would have been the perfect day for scrubbing my floors and for washing and hanging out the laundry. I had always been an energetic mother and liked a clean house, especially with a baby on the way. Thérèse and Aline were willing helpers; two of my uncles had sent them some weeks earlier so my children and I would not be alone without Charles.

But with all the recent happenings, I woke feeling overwhelmed, my mind tuned to an inner vibration – or was it a distant drumbeat? In this state, I could face only the most basic tasks. I tried to fix my mind on feeding eighteen-month Christian, four-year-old Charles-Vital, and the others in my apartment, and then on cleaning up after breakfast. I felt strung tight – listening, watching – and kept glancing out the window.

It was a relief, around eight o'clock, to see my friend Faina approaching, an empty basket on her head. She was a Hutu woman I had often prayed with. Her family was poorer than ours, yet she had a generous nature, and she came now to ask if I needed anything from the market in Nyakabuye. Touched by Faina's offer, I gave her enough money to buy cabbage, plums, bananas, and *lenga lenga*, a spinach-like vegetable. My heart lifted a little at her thoughtfulness – and at knowing that my household would have fresh food through the weekend.

Three hours later, Thomas, the Hutu leader of our prayer group, appeared at the gate. He told me he wanted to help out in these difficult times. After hesitating and shuffling his feet, he added that he would gladly hide any valuables for me, just in case there were . . . problems. His eyes never met mine, however, and his voice seemed unnaturally high-pitched. I thanked him but declined his offer.

At noon, it was time to prepare lunch, but, surprisingly, Faina had not yet returned with the fruit and vegetables. Twice I glanced up the road to see if she was coming. The third time I stepped out, I saw a figure in the distance, running our direction. It looked like Faina, but I had never known her to run, and this woman was empty-handed. As she came closer, I saw that it was indeed Faina – but she was almost unrecognizable. I hurried to meet her at the gate.

She was so upset and breathless, I could hardly make out her words: "Denise . . . your Aunt Priscilla . . . her two children . . . her father-in-law . . . terrible . . . in a ditch . . . Priscilla still alive . . .

asked for water . . . said to warn . . . killers coming . . . destroy all Tutsi!" Turning, Faina fled toward her own home.

I froze at her news. But I had to raise the alarm. Dashing through my house and out the back door, I cried, "Goretti, we are all about to die!"

She came running, and we met at the same spot where she had told me of the plane crash, nine days earlier. She was Catholic, I was Protestant, but such differences meant nothing – especially now. We embraced across the fence, saying goodbye, asking forgiveness for any way we might have hurt each other as neighbors.

Meanwhile, a confused hubbub was growing in the street as everyone in Bugarama – Tutsi and Hutu alike – rushed for home. Voices were shouting, "Interahamwe are coming! Interahamwe are coming!"

Darting inside and locking our doors, I called my household together in the corridor, where I hoped we might be safe from grenades.

"I sense that some of us will die today," I said, to a background of far-off shots and yells. "For those who are killed, *Rendez-vous au ciel* – we will meet in heaven." Kneeling in the hallway, we prayed aloud, asking God and each other for forgiveness.

Suddenly I heard a frenzied pounding at the gate. Had the attackers reached us so soon? But no, I could hear their shouts still at some distance.

Creeping to a window, I peeked between the drawn curtains. Flailing frantically was a boy I had never seen before. Manasseh hurried out and opened the gate, just enough for the boy to slip through, before relocking it.

The stranger stood panting in my corridor, the whites of his eyes betraying his fear – which only increased my own. Our group surrounded the boy, looking questioningly at him. Catching his breath, he said his name was Epa. He was seventeen. He had come to Bugarama to seek refuge with his aunt, down the street. But her Hutu husband had just ordered him to leave, pointing out my house as the nearest Tutsi home.

Epa was just in time. During our hasty exchange, the malicious shrieks had intensified. They were close . . . Then I heard Goretti's daughter Diane crying next door, and I knew the killers were upon us.

The terrifying noise of splintering wood and metal told me our iron-clad back door had given way. At their roar of entry, we scattered. I leapt for the bathroom, Christian on my back in his *ingobyi*.

The sounds that came through the bathroom door in the next minutes were unutterably horrible – savage roars, slashing metal, thumps, thuds, screams . . . I knew Christian and I, and my unborn child, would be next.

Where, oh where, is Charles-Vital? What is happening to him?

Certain there was no way to escape death now, I hurled a last desperate prayer at God: "Why didn't you tell me the truth? You promised to protect us, and now we are going to die! You have totally failed me!" My next thought was that we were about to enter heaven. My fear departed in that instant. I felt strong, ready to die. I straightened my shoulders and crossed my arms.

Just then, the locked doorknob rattled and a triumphant bellow burst through the thin wooden door. It took only seconds for the steel axe to crash through. Then five Interahamwe were crowding into the small space, getting in each other's way, peering at me.

One of the killers raised a dripping red blade. Contempt twisted his features, and his body gleamed with sweat. Grenades, hanging from his belt, clicked with every move, and strips of ammunition crossed his naked chest. But these fiends did not need bullets – they worked with steel.

"I'm going to kill you!" he gloated.

"Why?" I challenged.

"You Tutsi killed Burundi's president last year!" His accent told me he was Burundian.

"I had no part in that," I replied.

Another shoved forward, demanding, "Give us money!"

"It's in my bedroom."

Cursing, and tripping over each other, the five pushed their way back into the corridor. I passed between them, and they followed.

I entered my room. Anselm was curled on the floor behind the half-open door. His head was split open, and the wall behind was splashed with his blood. Beside him lay the girls. Aline looked dead, though I saw no wounds. Thérèse's body quivered and jerked. She was bleeding from deep gashes.

Under my pillow was the wallet that saved Christian and me, containing papers and 170,000 Rwandan francs, about $400. I gave it to the leader, who lost no time dividing the cash.

"Don't bother with her," he scoffed. "Let's get going!"

"She's a Tutsi – kill her!" another retorted, raising his machete. But the leader grasped his arm, pulling him out to continue their hunt. The others followed. Christian had remained motionless on my back.

I fainted to the floor.

When I came to, I had a split-second reprieve – thinking I was waking from a nightmare. But the sights and smells were all too real. I felt an instant's shocked amazement that I was alive. Then my thoughts flew to my four-year-old – where was he?

Charles-Vital was not among the dead and dying. Frantically, I searched the rooms for my child.

Stepping outdoors, I saw my houseboy, Samuel – and at his side stood my son. I swayed and almost collapsed again, from sheer relief at seeing him alive and unhurt.

Samuel, however, gestured madly, crying, "Go back inside! They said they would come back for you. I don't want to see them kill you!"

Swiftly passing little Christian to Samuel, I fled back indoors. Leaving my children tore me in two, but they had a better chance with my Hutu houseboy than with me.

I glanced around the apartment, but there was no adequate hiding place. Then I heard Manasseh's urgent whisper from my room, "Denise, here – crawl under the bed!"

It was dark down there. I tried to wedge myself sideways between the concrete floor and mattress board, but there was not enough space. My arm felt wet – and I realized I was lying in my relatives' blood. With the strength of desperation, I squeezed under the bed. I could feel every bone in my trembling body. The baby within kicked in protest.

Oh little one, will you live before you die? If only I could fly like a bird, airlifting my children to safety. . . .

I was breathing blood; its odor filled my mouth and nostrils. Horror, around and within me, was swamping clear thought. How I yearned for Charles, his reassurance, his common sense. What was happening to him? He could swim, I recalled, with my first twinge of hope in hours. Maybe he would escape across Lake Kivu, join my parents in the Congo . . .

Manasseh's back was pressed against mine, and I sensed his terror. He had seen and heard even more than I had. His teeth were chattering, and occasional spasms convulsed his body. Like him, I knew the killers would return. Without doubt they would find us in their macabre game of hide-and-seek, and then . . .

But I mustn't panic, can't let fear paralyze my mind. For my children's sake, I must collect my wits.

Where were my sons now? I had given them to Samuel's care; with his childish ways, he had seemed almost a third son to me, and I had always trusted him with my boys. But in this crazy new world, might even he turn against us?

I was tempted to sneak outdoors to reunite with my children and escape this trap – but Manasseh insisted that leaving the house would be suicide. Interahamwe were swarming the area like wasps.

"Jesus of Nazareth, help me!"

Thérèse's voice . . . Oh God, she is still alive! This is terrible . . . What can I do? Death is encircling us, constricting, tightening . . . I feel its breath, hear its hiss.

"Jesus of Nazareth, come help!" Thérèse's repeated cry turned to a moan, then faded away . . . Silence.

Suddenly I detected a faint jangling sound – or had I imagined it? "What's that?" I asked in alarm.

"It's Epa, in the closet," Manasseh whispered. "They didn't find him."

Epa . . . I had forgotten him.

I felt a brief stab of relief that I had refused to shelter Francine – otherwise she and her children, too, would now be lying, mangled, on my floor.

Hours passed. Darkness came, hiding the ghastly tableau in my home and in countless Tutsi homes throughout our town and across Rwanda.

With nightfall, Interahamwe took a break from their gruesome labor. I could hear their bragging from the bar across the road. Some were voices I heard every Saturday night; others were strange. With a fresh pang of fear, I recognized the Burundi accent I had heard at noon. Was it the killer I had confronted?

From my awkward position under the bed, I caught fragments of their boasts. "Cockroach" was the word I heard most: I slit *inyenzi's* throat . . . cut her in pieces . . . stuck him up on a pole . . . hung him . . . clubbed her to death . . .

Occasionally a snatch of drunken singing reached my ears; RTLM's catchy hate songs matched the killers' mood. They must have been consuming immense quantities of beer, but I had no doubt that the next day they would be sober enough to carry on.

They don't drink to work up nerve to kill – they drink to celebrate how systematically they've done it.

One man was so loud, his remarks carried distinctly across the road: "We will exterminate every last cockroach, no matter where they hide! Our children will ask, 'What's a Tutsi?' and we will tell of an extinct tribe, a people of the past!"

The raucous cheers and rough laughter continued hour after hour. Exhausted, I finally dozed off. . .

I snapped awake. I had heard my name. ". . . Denise Uwimana. Manasseh must be somewhere too. We'll find them both, no problem. Tomorrow they die!"

Now that I was alert, I realized with dismay that something besides their words had wakened me. My discomfort was more than my strained position; the wetness I felt was more than the blood on the floor. My waters had broken.

Within me, steady pressure was building, then receding . . . and again. I had to face the fact that I was in labor – that in a matter of hours, my baby would be born.

Oh little one, you could not have chosen a worse moment in the entire history of the world . . .

With effort, I pulled myself from under the bed and managed to stand upright. The pale bedside clock told me it was three o'clock in the morning.

"Manasseh, help me," I called. "I need to get out of here!"

I begged him to fetch Marcel, the clinic director living next door. Surely he would come to assist with the birth.

Cautiously Manasseh crept outside, but he returned immediately, whispering, "Denise, I can't reach Marcel without being seen. There are Interahamwe all around his house."

Creeping to a window, I saw with shock that all the lights were on in Goretti and Viateur's half of the next-door duplex, their windows bare of curtains. Their apartment was being ransacked. At that moment, a fellow employee walked out their door, a mattress balanced on his head. Where were Goretti and Viateur and their three children, Fiston, Kim, and Diane?

I realized Manasseh was right about the danger, and I knew from the militants' words that they were hunting him. Many were his coworkers. If they sighted him, it would be the end.

On Friday – less than two days previous, but seeming eons ago – Manasseh had cut a hole in the fence dividing my backyard from the Chinese employees' property. Since their departure, their grounds were no longer patrolled. We two now crept through this opening to hide in their banana grove.

But this was no place to give birth – outside, in the dark, with no one to help! Then Madame Kibuye sprang to mind, in the other half of my own duplex. She and her husband were Hutu . . . but he was probably outdoors with all the other Hutu men; perhaps she would have pity. It was a drastic risk, but she was my only hope.

Manasseh and I squeezed back into my backyard. Since the Kibuyes shared our building, there was only a light reed fence separating my yard from theirs, and Manasseh now lifted this partition. Stooping once more, I crept into the Kibuyes' yard and stole to their back door. I gave a sharp rap, then another.

"Who's there?" Madame Kibuye sounded alarmed.

My heart pounding, I identified myself.

"Denise! You're alive? After that racket through the wall?" Her words came fast. "But I can't let you in – Interahamwe would kill me!"

With the last dim hope extinguished, my mind went blank. I could not think. I could not reply. I did not move.

Moments passed. Then the door opened a crack. Madame Kibuye peered out. "Is the baby coming?"

I nodded dumbly. She hesitated a moment longer, then leaned out and yanked me inside.

"They're looking for you," she hissed. "If they find you here, they'll kill me too!" She pushed me into her guest room, where I dropped to the bed.

During the next hour, Madame Kibuye darted in and out several times, wringing her hands, entreating me to go. I did not respond. My contractions had become insistent, urgent. Holding in my screams took all my willpower.

Around 4:30, I started hearing the unmistakable voices of militants from the street. Madame Kibuye dashed back into the room once more, now almost crazy with fear.

"Get out of my house!" she implored.

"I can't!" My pains were excruciating, nearing the climax.

Suddenly she grabbed three or four stools, stacking them in the corridor beneath a ceiling trapdoor.

"Quick, hide in the attic!"

I stared at her in disbelief.

"Look at me," I gasped. "My child is coming!"

Madame Kibuye knew I was right, but she was beside herself, repeating, "They will kill me! They will kill me!"

Through the wall, from my apartment, I heard voices and scraping, dragging sounds; looters had moved in. My neighbors, helping themselves . . . We had gotten out just in time.

Then everything happened fast. Madame Kibuye did her best to help. In a matter of minutes, my baby was born. My physical agony was over.

As if sensing the danger, my newborn son cried just once, to open his lungs – but not long or loud enough to attract the killers, already busy this early Sunday morning.

Madame Kibuye ran out to her kitchen hut and returned with a knife, its blade sticky from trimming banana bunches. Not pausing to clean it, she cut the cord.

"Now go!" she whispered. "Quick!"

I tried to stand. But I was dizzy and had to sit down.

Just then the back door opened, and Manasseh slipped in. With the dawning of day, he had left his scant hiding place among the banana trees. Glancing around, he saw the stacked stools. Like a monkey, he disappeared into the attic.

But what could I do? I could not climb up there with my baby. And from the sounds in the street, I believed the militia would enter any moment.

Then I had an idea. The Kibuyes' apartment mirrored my own. Stumbling into their storeroom, I hid behind the door – pulling it open as wide as possible behind me. Crouched behind the partially open door, I nursed my infant to keep him still.

From this cramped position, I could hear Cimerwa's gardener, Harorimana, addressing a crowd outside.

"Who do these children belong to?" he was asking.

My heart skipped a beat as I heard the answering chorus: "Those are Denise Uwimana's boys!"

"Keep an eye on those two," Harorimana commanded. Then he continued, "Has anyone hidden in Kibuye's house?"

"No, no one," came the response.

Seemingly dissatisfied, Harorimana repeated, "Does anybody know if a Tutsi has hidden in this apartment?"

Silence. Then I heard a woman's voice: "I saw Manasseh disappear inside."

In seconds, militia and others forced their way in. They piled past the storeroom, blind to my baby and me behind the door.

From the guest room, someone exclaimed, "What happened here?"

None of the people who had entered seemed able or willing to answer.

The hunt continued. Then came a triumphant whoop. One of the men had noticed the stools stacked beneath the attic trapdoor.

"Somebody climbed up here! Who's up there?"

"It must be Manasseh!" another yelled. "Manasseh, come down!"

Silence.

A hubbub of disputing voices broke out, interrupted by a terse command: "Everyone out!"

When they had all left the building, a grenade was tossed in.

From my hiding place, I saw it hit and bounce across the floor. Shielding my child with my body, I held my breath, waiting for the explosion.

Seconds passed.

Then came a disgusted outburst. "Don't you even know how to set off a grenade?"

The retort was equally annoyed. "Shut up! Sometimes they don't work. I'll try another."

A second grenade flew through the air and landed with a thud. My eyes were shut tight as I clutched my son, but I heard its rattle as it rolled toward us. Again I waited, waited . . . but this, too, was a dud.

People started shouting, some blaming the thrower, others demanding that Manasseh be forcibly taken from the attic.

A strident voice instructed, "Madame Kibuye, don't let Manasseh escape. We're getting more equipment."

I heard the tramp and scuffle of feet, the clamor retreating.

Madame Kibuye appeared immediately at my hiding place. Frantically, she whispered that the crowd had gone but would be back – and she didn't know what to do with me. I realized she was too distraught to think clearly. It was up to me to forge a plan.

"Can you let me into your kitchen hut?" I asked. "And please, may I have some clean clothes?"

Passing me her shabbiest *kitenge*, she stepped out to make sure the militia and mob were really gone. By the time I was dressed, she was back.

"No one's watching – all the stragglers are busy looting your apartment. Come!"

She led me quickly out the back door and into her kitchen hut, where she spread a plastic sack over the ashes in the fire pit. "Lie there," she said.

My baby slept, a picture of peace. But I could not relax, exhausted though I was. Fear kept me on high alert, my ears strained to identify any noise, while tormenting thoughts and images whirled through my mind.

From a crack in the hut's wall, I could see what was happening in the road; I helplessly watched the gang return after half an hour, with weapons, ladder, and flashlight, determined to flush my cousin from the attic.

Excited onlookers milled around, including Madame Kibuye and all the Hutu neighbors. Then I noticed a knot of women to one side. They were whispering and glancing toward the kitchen hut. My friend Josephine was among them – except I no longer knew if I had any friends. Abruptly, she left the cluster and walked up to the mayor.

"Denise Uwimana has just had her baby," Josephine said boldly. "Do not kill her!"

"What? Denise is alive?" He sounded incredulous. Then, inexplicably, he asked a soldier to take me and my newborn to Cimerwa's clinic around the corner.

Josephine and several others marched up to my hiding place. The kitchen door swung open.

"Come!" the soldier commanded.

I did not know what would happen next. I knew only that I was in their hands, at their mercy. I was too fatigued, physically and mentally, to even think about attempting escape.

Out on the road, I found myself facing a noisy throng of colleagues and neighbors, mingled with outsiders. And in front stood Charles-Vital and Christian, holding Samuel's hands.

Seeing me the same instant, they called, "Mama, Mama!"

"Hey," a stranger suggested, "let's shoot them in front of their mother!"

"Yes, yes," others agreed lustily. "Shoot them in front of their mother!"

An argument broke out: Were the boys really mine, or did they belong to Josephine or one of the other Hutu ladies standing around?

A shout diverted their attention. Interahamwe were dragging Manasseh from the Kibuyes' house. My sons took that moment to dash to my side.

The men were armed with rifles, machetes, axes, hammers, pickaxes, and nail-studded clubs. They made Manasseh remove his watch. Then they told him to take off his shirt. His shaking hands could hardly undo the buttons.

As soon as his shirt and watch had been passed to one killer, another knocked Manasseh to the ground with a cruel cudgel blow. Then, with a swift, practiced stroke, another cut off his head.

Blackness threatened my vision.

Manasseh! You and I played together as kids; you sang with me in the church choir; you walked with Charles to protect him from harm . . . I never dreamed I would see you killed . . .

My legs buckled. Firmly, Josephine took the baby from my arms, while two women grabbed my elbows.

Following the soldier, our group set off toward the health center, about two hundred yards' walk. Did my children and I stand a chance of survival, I wondered as we stumbled along with our captors, or had our death merely been postponed?

Suddenly half a dozen Interahamwe, some disguised with banana leaves, broke from the brush beside the road. Dusty from the hunt, they yelled exultantly and swung their weapons in grim gestures of victory – for they were pulling Francine, her baby on her back and her older child clutching her hand. The wild band had ferreted these three from a cassava field and were clearly aching for the kill as they steered Francine toward us.

Francine – your husband begged me to shelter you and your little ones!

The same instant, Celestin appeared along the road from the opposite direction. Broad and muscular, formerly active in MRND, he had left politics because of the rising extremism and had become a confessing Christian.

Confronting the leader of the young militants, he asked, "What are you doing with that woman?"

"We found her and her little cockroaches hiding in a field. Now we'll execute them, like the others!"

"Why didn't you kill them in the field?" Celestin demanded.

"We were going to, but when we saw this soldier with these others, we thought . . ."

"You thought nothing at all!" Celestin interrupted. "You can't kill them here! Leave it to me. Your captives are coming with us."

His authority must have impressed them. Resentfully, the young men shoved Francine toward us and disappeared into the trees to continue their grisly search.

I was flooded with relief – but just then, I heard a vicious uproar behind us. The horde had discovered seventeen-year-old Epa in my bedroom closet. Shouting that they knew he was Tutsi from the ID card they had found in his shoe, they dragged him into the street.

I pressed my children's faces against myself. I could not bear for them to see Epa beheaded.

THIS IS ONLY a tiny window into the genocide against the Tutsi, a few hours from one personal perspective.

How could ordinary people veer from a normal life – looking for work, studying at college, or earning a living – to butchering others?

I can only answer that demons from hell were unleashed like seething lava over our land. Not the comic-scary hobgoblins of my mother's legends, but cosmic forces before which human beings are dust specks in a volcanic explosion.

That is not to say that individuals don't count. I believe that each one murdered was welcomed into the next world, just as I believe that each who survived was saved for a reason.

We who lived faced a harsher task; I often felt death would have been preferable. How hard it has been, through grueling years:

to overcome the loss, battle to forgive, and then bring healing to others – yes, even to killers. They, too, were specks of dust.

In the West, many people scoff at the idea of invisible spiritual powers. I'm sure some of these skeptics would acknowledge the reality of such powers, however, if they had been caught in a firestorm like ours. United Nations general Roméo Dallaire wrote, "In Rwanda I shook hands with the devil. I have seen him, I have smelled him, and I have touched him. I know the devil exists, and therefore I know there is a God."

I believe each of us plays a role in this spiritual war, and each soul decides to serve life or death. There is no neutral. Death had a grip on Rwanda in 1994, but it has a grip in other places, too, and has other weapons besides machetes and grenades.

Also, although a plummeting plane ignited our inferno, the tinder had been accumulating a long time: division, envy, hatred, and the labeling of Tutsi as vermin. For the rest of my life, I will protest the least insinuation that any person or group of people is less than human.

9

Haven

IT TOOK ONLY MINUTES to reach the factory grounds with our armed escort. The Cimerwa guard on duty opened the gate, and we proceeded to the health center. As we stepped through the door, I realized its rooms were already occupied by other trauma-tized women and children. Marcel, who ran the infirmary, ushered us into a room.

Entering, I saw Goretti and her daughter Diane on one of the beds. I had believed them dead. A deep gash crossed Goretti's forehead, and Diane's upper arm was bandaged. Pulling herself together, Goretti told me that twelve-year-old Kim had managed to escape. But the attackers had killed her husband, Viateur, and then their fourteen-year-old son, Fiston – after cutting off his arms.

Oh Goretti – your firstborn son! And your steady, warm-hearted husband! If only Viateur had stayed in Burundi when he took the Chinese workers there four days ago. If only he'd used that chance to smuggle his family to safety . . .

Oscar and Consolée, to whom I owed so much, had been slain with one of their six children. Their three remaining daughters – Furaha, Mapendo, and three-year-old Ruth – were among the survivors in the clinic. (Two young sons were away from home at the time of the attack and, I later learned, also survived.)

Despite a deep machete wound on her head, fifteen-year-old Furaha spoke to me: "When Interahamwe entered our street yesterday, our father told us to pray for our murderers, because that's what Jesus did. He also told us to pray for you, Denise, because your husband, Charles, was gone. As we finished praying, they broke down our door . . ."

Furaha had lain unconscious under corpses on the Daihatsu Transporter. As the cleanup team threw the bodies into the river, she revived and begged for water. The crew foreman – a former colleague of her father's – told the others not to throw her in alive. Instead, they brought her to join her younger sisters in the infirmary.

Midafternoon, the clinic's calm was shattered. Yussuf Munyakazi was out of town this weekend, spearheading a massacre in Nyamasheke, as I later learned. But when his Bugarama cohort learned that I had had my baby, that my children and I had been allowed to live, and that we were in the factory's health center, they were incensed and sent one of their number to finish us off. He entered – a big, strong man, machete in hand.

"Where's the woman who had the baby?" he demanded.

I was lying on the bed with my children. "Here I am," I said.

"Boy or girl?"

From the corner of my eye, I saw Goretti on the other bed, urgently signaling me to say "girl." She knew too well that males were the primary target. But I was sure we were all about to be killed anyway, and didn't want my last words to be a lie.

"He's a boy," I whispered, clutching him to my chest.

"Ah!" breathed the killer, stepping closer, raising his

blood-stained blade. "You know what we did three days ago in Mukoma? Killed every last baby boy! Made the mothers watch!"

I gasped, and he swung. But – as if a stronger hand had grabbed his wrist – his stroke caught in midair. The man took a step back.

His eyes shifted to Charles-Vital.

"He's a boy!" he exclaimed. "I'll end him with one blow!"

Again he raised his arm and swung. Again his stroke broke mid-swing . . . Advancing on Christian, he did the same – with the same result.

Dropping his arm, he looked around at the women and girls.

"You know what else we did in Mukoma?" he leered. "We killed all *inyenzi* men and raped their womenfolk!"

A thrust of his machete emphasized his intent.

"Please, no!" Goretti cried. "I am pregnant and injured. My daughter is only eleven. My friend Denise had a baby today – and Francine gave birth three weeks ago. Have mercy!"

I was amazed at Goretti's courage. I could not speak.

His eyes roved over us. He pointed his weapon at Diane. "I'll take that one!"

I was paralyzed, hardly breathing – but silently praying, "God, please let me be killed without being raped."

Then, inexplicably, the brute tottered and look confused, as if all strength and determination were draining out of him. With an abrupt change of approach, he said, "Give me money!"

We had nothing and told him so.

"I'll be back at six o'clock," he declared. "If you have no money at six, I'll kill you all then."

He left.

Goretti flew to Marcel's office, begging him to hurry to Ezekias, the Hutu Catholic who had helped Joram escape. Marcel went immediately. Ezekias, too, wasted no time, sending Marcel back with cash. When our predator returned at six o'clock, Goretti gave him six thousand francs. Snatching it, he disappeared.

Later that evening, a man limped up to the infirmary door, three shell-shocked little girls clinging to his side. His name was Simpunga. He and his wife, Marguerite, both Cimerwa colleagues, had been personal friends. When my husband was in prison, they had brought money to help me through; and when Charles was released, they had been the first to visit us. Now Marguerite was dead, murdered. Marcel led Simpunga and his daughters to the room next to the one I shared with Goretti, Francine, and our children.

The building became quiet. Finally, I could settle my children for the night and try to get some rest myself. How long was it since I had slept? Had my baby really been born just this morning? Today felt a thousand years long.

I closed my eyes, bone-weary and soul-shaken – yet awed by God's protection. What had arrested the killer's hand? Across my mind flashed a childhood memory: an angel's flaming sword barring evil from our door, an invisible ring of fire keeping harm away.

It had been when my family lived in Kalambi, the primitive jungle village in the Congo. One afternoon my parents had noticed an oddly tied bundle of grass in their bedroom. Papa asked if we kids knew who had put it there. We did not.

A few days later, a spiral strip of metal coiled around a pearl appeared in their room. Again none of us knew where it came from.

When Papa found this second strange object, he went to the hospital warden, who said he had seen such things in the hands of people repenting of involvement in witchcraft. Papa called one such woman.

"These fetishes should have killed you!" she burst out when she saw them. "Your God must be fighting for you!"

She insisted that they be destroyed, so Papa burned them.

Later, at church, someone told my parents that after Papa got rid of the fetishes, sorceresses planned another way to hurt our family;

but when they had crept to our house that night, they had seen an angel blocking our door, sword in hand. One, in a last attempt to curse us, returned the following night. This time she saw our house surrounded by a moat of fire – which no one else saw – and she abandoned her plan.

My mind returned to the present.

Yes, God protected us today. But what will tonight bring? Or tomorrow? And what about the ones who died today – why didn't God protect them?

It was a long and terrible night, but toward morning I finally drifted off.

I was wakened, as daylight brightened, by the ominous tread of marching feet. Peeking out, I saw a phalanx of Interahamwe approaching our hideout. This was no disorderly mob like I'd seen outside Madame Kibuye's the day before. This regiment moved and stopped with disciplined precision. At their head was the killer to whom we had given six thousand francs the night before.

Other people must have heard them. A crowd was starting to gather. Simpunga, too, looked fearfully out his window.

"Yussuf Munyakazi's skilled assassins. Coming for me." He spoke in quiet resignation, but a sob caught his voice.

The leader now addressed his troops. "Leave the women and children. See who else is in there."

Three militants strode to the door and entered. Walking down the hall, they glanced into each room until they reached Simpunga's. Seizing him, they dragged him out. A clamor erupted from the bystanders.

"It's Simpunga!"

"Kill him, kill him, kill him!"

I don't know where Simpunga's captors put him, but that night they brought him back and killed him outside the clinic. We women inside heard their devilish shrieks, the sickening sound of blades cleaving flesh and bone, Simpunga's screams of terror and pain. We suffered every moment of his death.

In the days that followed, two more women, Pascasie and Azera, were brought to the clinic and joined us in our room. Pascasie was pregnant with her first child; her husband, Samuel, had just been killed. We were now fourteen people sharing a small room with only two beds. A bucket served as a toilet because it was too dangerous to go out.

Ten years later, Yussuf Munyakazi – the oldest person charged with genocide crimes – was found and arrested where he had been hiding in the Congo, disguised as an imam. The International Criminal Tribunal for Rwanda, based in Arusha, Tanzania, sentenced him to twenty-five years in prison for his involvement in the deaths of five thousand civilian Tutsi.

Yet that five thousand did not include people like Simpunga, killed by the men Yussuf had trained. God alone knows their number.

NOT EVERY HUTU wanted us dead. All of us Tutsi who found refuge in the health center owe our lives to courageous Hutu neighbors who risked everything to help us. Even a Cimerwa guard showed compassion, when he lent me his Bible. I don't think any of them knew what the others were doing for us. It was best that way.

Marcel, who ran the infirmary, allowed us mothers and children to stay there. He went beyond what Cimerwa officials permitted, to make life bearable for us.

Celestin, who had rescued Francine and her children, regularly frequented the bars where Interahamwe met, to eavesdrop on their discussions and learn their plans. He and his wife, Thérèse, brought us food, even in times of acute danger. Most of their friends and relatives spurned them because of their kindness to Tutsi.

Mukashyaka was another brave soul. She regularly sent their six-year-old son, Toto, to bring us food, even after her husband found out and demanded she stop.

One day I asked the child how he managed to evade the militia.

"That's easy," he grinned. "I hug the pot of food with one arm, like this. With my other hand, I roll my wheel down the road with my stick, like this."

Dramatically, he re-enacted the scene.

"All the guys are watching me. Then, when they look the other way, I pop into the clinic."

Toto burst out laughing. His plucky spirit did us as much good as the food he brought.

My colleague Annemarie remained loyal. So did her husband, Saidi. They brought clothes for Christian and Charles-Vital, diapers for the baby, and even a small hotplate, so I could cook. They occasionally sent money as well. And they paid a young Hutu girl, Charlotte, to bring food to the clinic after dark and help with the laundry. She always left before daybreak so as not to be seen.

Another Hutu couple risked their lives to save ours: Louitpold and Josephine. She was the one who had told the mayor to spare me, and then carried my newborn to the clinic after I was taken from Madame Kibuye's kitchen hut.

Josephine and her husband had moved to Bugarama from Kigali in 1990. Since they happened to arrive shortly before the RPF invasion, they were viewed with suspicion and, like Charles, they were arrested that October, accused of being infiltrators – even though they were Hutu. They had been jailed locally, rather than in Cyangugu Prison, and were soon released on Casimir's orders; Louitpold being a mechanic, Cimerwa had missed his services.

Josephine and Louitpold became Christians soon after that. Once Charles was released from prison, he and I had visited their home. For years, they had spent most of their money on fetish treatments, believing Louitpold's epilepsy resulted from sorcery. As a result, they still lived in poverty. In spite of that, Josephine had prepared Charles and me a lavish meal.

Decades on, Josephine and her husband are still looking after
people in need; at present, that means growing corn and beans for
hospital patients who can't afford to buy food. That is just how they
cared for us Tutsi in the clinic during the genocide.

Louitpold came as often as he could, telling us that God was
with us and that there were people praying for us. He brought a
small transistor radio, charging me to keep it well hidden. He also
brought food. One day he was observed; on his way home, Hutu
militia intercepted him and beat him to the ground. Pressing a
blade to his throat, they threatened to kill him if he ever helped us
again. But Louitpold was not deterred. He was simply more careful
the next time.

One morning I heard light footsteps approaching the health
center – a woman. As always, we held our breath, because anyone
entering could bring danger. But it was Josephine.

"Denise," she called, "your baby needs his vaccinations." Vaccinations would mean going to Mashesha, and we both knew I would
be killed if I stepped outside the factory gate. I thought Josephine
was crazy, and told her so.

"No, Denise, not you," she responded. "*I* will take him to be
vaccinated. Trust me!"

I was filled with doubt; the hazards were great. Yet I knew the
value of vaccinations – particularly if we should end up in a refugee
camp, where epidemics spread fast and infants are the first to die.
Josephine had certainly proved herself reliable . . .

I gave her my baby. She strapped him to her back, hiding him
as best she could under her *kitenge*. As she walked out the gate, I
dropped to the bed and buried my face.

Three hours passed – feeling like three days – before Josephine
returned. Placing my son in my arms, she sat down to describe her
excursion:

When I got near the barricade, I was scared.

"Jesus," I prayed, "there's a roadblock on the bridge. What shall

I tell them when they see this baby? Please don't let me down."

Among the sentries, I recognized some from the cement plant and some from our church youth group. One of them challenged me.

"You, woman," he said, "where are you going?"

"I've had my baby," I told him, "and I'm going to Mashesha for his vaccinations."

"You're lying!" he said. "You're still pregnant. This is the child of a Tutsi snake!"

"No, this is my child!" I cried. "You'll have to kill me before you harm him!"

The militia started arguing. Then one of them said, "Come on, Josephine, you know this is a Tutsi child. When the snake is full grown, it will bite you."

But when I stood my ground, they let me pass.

I arrived in Mashesha. The midwife in charge refused to care for your baby – even though she used to sing in the church choir with you! She said, "There are no more Tutsi in Rwanda! Why do you want to help this child?"

Luckily her helper agreed to vaccinate your son. So here he is, safe and sound . . .

When Josephine and Louitpold's daughter was born after the genocide, they named her Sauvée, "Saved one."

Years later, I asked this couple why they risked their lives for us Tutsi, when almost everyone else joined the killing.

"Ever since I found forgiveness of my sins at the cross, I vowed never to betray Jesus again," Louitpold answered.

A FEW DAYS after our arrival in the health center, my baby developed an infection, because of the dirty knife Madame Kibuye had used to cut his cord. I knocked at Marcel's office door and asked him to examine my child.

"Name of infant?" Marcel asked.

Haven

Everyone in the clinic had been pestering me about what I would call my baby. They all said he was a miracle child. I had to agree, certain our lives had been spared on his account – that seeing a newborn had touched our neighbors' humanity. But I had not yet chosen a name, and Marcel knew it.

"He has no name," I replied. I couldn't help remembering the Interahamwe who had come to the door and jeeringly suggested I call the baby Rusigajiki, which means "death has taken everything."

Without looking up from the form he was filling out, Marcel wrote "Niyonkuru."

Thus the matter was resolved, and my son was named Niyonkuru, "God is great." Christian, however, simply called his new brother Petit, "the little one" – and that's the name that stuck.

Even though a dozen or more of us had taken refuge in the health center, it was still serving its purpose as infirmary for everyone connected with Cimerwa. The daily comings and goings were unnerving, keeping us mothers on edge.

After Marcel locked up and went home at the end of each day, I would bring the radio out of hiding and tune in to the BBC or to Radio Muhabura, the RPF station. That's how I learned that the liberation army – as we Tutsi called the RPF – was gaining ground in Rwanda, particularly in the north and east.

One day the BBC stated that people in Uganda and Tanzania were reporting innumerable bodies floating downriver from Rwanda to Lake Victoria. Horror rose within me, swiftly followed by wrath.

Yes, you Interahamwe might kill us all – but the RPF is coming! They will avenge us! They will kill you too!

Radio Muhabura often played the RPF anthem, to encourage any surviving Tutsi. The song had the opposite effect on me. I imagined the freedom fighters arriving in the southwest to find us all dead. My brother Fidel had joined the RPF, and I was sure I would never see him again.

87

We women and children in the health center had become some-thing of a curiosity for our Hutu neighbors, who would wander by to catch a glimpse of living Tutsi.

Since the factory was still closed for the official period of mourning the president, Bugarama's youth were idle – when not on the rampage. Their chief pastime was hanging out with Intera-hamwe outside the vacant factory. Sometimes they hardly budged from outside its gates for days. It was almost impossible for us to receive food at those times, and our children cried with hunger.

The militants, lounging in front of the factory gates, were just waiting for their superiors' order to kill the clinic's occupants. They loudly described their latest exploits, to impress bystanders and to taunt us Tutsi survivors.

One day they described my grandparents' region where, they bragged, Interahamwe decapitated Tutsi and took their heads to the provincial capital, Cyangugu. They made sure I knew that my father's parents, Tateh Ephraim and Tateh Damaris, had been beheaded along with most of Papa's brothers and many of their neighbors.

I later learned that my father's sister Domitilla, with her husband and seven children, had drowned themselves in Lake Kivu to escape this fate.

Occupying my children was a challenge. Eleven-year-old Diane, who had always been a cheerful playmate and depend-able babysitter, was suffering from the terrible wound on her shoulder – and even more, from witnessing the brutal deaths of her father and oldest brother. Simpunga's daughters were locked in their anguish, as were Oscar and Consolée's girls. Goretti had been severely injured, and Francine had her own little ones to care for. So, although I was recovering from giving birth, it was up to me to look after my boys.

One morning, while I was caring for my newborn, four-year-old Charles-Vital slipped outside when the gate was opened for a patient. Pleased to be outdoors again, he started playing in the road – contented, unaware that a teenager had noticed and was beckoning Interahamwe to come and kill him.

I was oblivious of my child's peril. But Marcel, who happened to glance out the window, grasped the situation instantly. Dashing out, he grabbed my son and pulled him back inside.

"Don't you *ever* go out there again!" he scolded Charles-Vital, giving him a shake.

Sometimes the housegirl, Charlotte, played with my boys at night or rocked Petit to sleep. Her crooning one evening – "Such a darling baby! Too bad you're a cockroach!" – was yet one more jolting reminder to be vigilant.

One day we heard shouts outside the gate and caught the name "Kim" in the uproar. Goretti had been desperate with worry about her twelve-year-old son, who had escaped the attack on her house. Now it seemed Interahamwe had captured him.

Marcel strode out the door to the gate. I never learned how he achieved it, but in minutes he was back with Goretti's son. Kim was shaking and sobbing; I tried to distract my sons, to give him some privacy with his mother and sister. A few hours later, for his safety and ours, Marcel helped him escape to another location.

The next day, Goretti told me how Kim had cheated death on April 16. One of the killers had asked him where his father kept the family's money. Kim told the man to follow, leading him slowly away from the house – then dodging and sprinting off before the man could catch him.

I tried to shield my sons from the carnage outside, but they saw too much. One day Charles-Vital asked, "Mama, is this the end of the world?"

From the window he had seen the Daihatsu piled with bodies. Bugarama's mayor had ordered that they be collected from Tutsi homes and from the streets, to be dumped in the river. I assailed heaven.

Oh God, when these people stand before your throne of judgment, when they ask where you were when they needed you, how will you answer? What will you say to the little children who don't know why they had to die? What will you say to their killers?

Bugarama's Interahamwe kept a list, ticking off names as local Tutsi men were eliminated. They had started using dogs to find any still hiding. At night they would gather in Casimir's bar to tell their stories, rank who had killed most, and compare methods.

During the day, I concentrated on caring for my children and the others around me. At night, though, my thoughts would fly to Charles. Not knowing what had happened to him – or might still be happening – was agony. But I would not admit that he could be dead, that I might even now be a widow.

After all, widows are old women. I was still in my twenties.

10

Alone

MY THREE SMALL SONS and I stayed in Cimerwa's health center for nearly six weeks, an emotionally draining time fraught with anxiety, tension, and heartbreak.

Fear was our constant companion, and I never got used to it. Some days, it turned to panic.

April 23 was such a day. That evening I saw a militant approaching: Wasi Wasi, who had been Manasseh's coworker. I tried to read his face when he got close. Was he coming to rape? To kill? I saw no lust in his eyes . . . He carried no weapon . . .

Stopping at the entrance, he called, "Hey, Tutsi refugees!"

I stepped to the door. "What do you want?" I asked.

"All remaining Tutsi are about to be taken to Cyangugu," he replied. "You will all be killed there, in Kamarampaka Stadium."

Appalled, I asked, "Why are you telling us this?"

"Well, I don't want them to kill you. Think up some excuse – don't go with them."

Why would he warn us? I wondered. Had his heart softened? Anyway, there was nothing we could do to prevent whatever might happen next.

The next day several officials came to register the clinic's occupants. Sebatware was one of them. Looking around curiously, he probed, "How do you survive in this place? What do you eat?"

None of us responded or even caught each other's eye. We weren't about to hint that his wife, Daphrose, regularly sent us food, from his own table!

After recording our names, the men left. Questions buzzed through my brain like the ever-present flies.

Are they planning to take us to the stadium, as Wasi Wasi said? When? Will we really be killed there?

Nothing happened that day, or the next, or the next. Time crawled, as we lingered in death's waiting room.

Finally, on Friday, April 29, a truck pulled up and parked outside the factory gate – our transport to Kamarampaka Stadium. The mayor arrived and read out the names of everyone meant to board the vehicle – all of us in the health center.

That very morning, however, Charles-Vital had come down with dysentery. And when the mayor called my name, Marcel said, "Denise Uwimana cannot go. Her son is sick."

No one contradicted him. The truck drove off without us.

Never had I felt so alone, so vulnerable, as I did that day after the truck vanished from view. As hours, then days, dragged by, I missed the comradeship of Goretti, Francine, Pascasie, Azera, Oscar and Consolée's girls, and the other children. What was happening to them? What would happen to us?

Oh God, how have we Tutsi sinned that we must die like this? We are no different from others. Why, Lord, why?

Psalms expressed my feelings: "My tears have been my meat day and night, while they continually say unto me, Where is thy God?"

Oh Lord, where are you? Why don't you intervene? Don't you see how women, and innocent little girls, are raped? Don't you see how Hutu slaughter our people? How dogs eat the flesh of the dead?

Bitterness gnawed at my gut when I thought of our church elders. It must have been to people like them that Jesus said, "Not everyone who says, 'Lord, Lord,' will enter my kingdom." These pious Christians had refused, out of fear, to take in Oscar and Consolée's girls, even though Oscar had been the most active, faithful brother in our church.

Soon it seemed all of Bugarama was aware that only my children and I had stayed in Cimerwa's health center. I felt our danger keenly. Interahamwe outside the gate made nasty comments, purposely loud so I would hear.

"Let's keep Denise alive – she can become our woman!"

"Shall we kill the little boys now – or wait till they're older, so they understand why they have to die?"

"Denise, have you heard? The UN has pulled out of Rwanda – no one cares what happens to you Tutsi!"

Nights were the worst, when I lay on the bed, listening. A rustling outside might be an animal – or an assassin. Dozing off, I seemed to hear voices whispering, "We know where you are, Denise. You won't escape us!" Nightmares plagued me: Interahamwe breaking into the clinic and torturing my children . . . When my own screams woke me, my pulse was racing and my clothes were drenched in sweat.

During the day, my thoughts often turned to my fellow survivors – would they make it through? Would we?

Oh Goretti, how are you? Has your fatherless baby been born?

Late one afternoon in mid-May, I received an official visit from Cimerwa's directors. All three belonged to MRND, the party that orchestrated the genocide against the Tutsi. Gasasira did not directly participate in murder, but Casimir is now in prison and Sebatware fled Rwanda and is still a fugitive from justice.

When I saw these three approaching, from the window, I had
no idea how involved in the killing each of them was. I knew only
that my survival was an embarrassment to them, especially as I
inhabited their own health center. My palms became damp and my
throat constricted as they walked in.

Sebatware began. "Why are you still in the infirmary?" he asked
sternly. "Are you sick?"

"No." *Why is he faking ignorance?*

"Why didn't you join your *inyenzi* relations?" Casimir
demanded.

No one insulting my loved ones gets an answer from me! I kept my
mouth shut.

"We want you out of here in two days," Casimir concluded.
"Either join your relatives, or go to Nyarushishi Refugee Camp."

It was a dire moment. I would never voluntarily take my children to the camp at Nyarushishi, certain the place was a death
trap. As for relatives, had any survived? I believed my parents were
still alive in the Congo – but the three directors knew as well as I
did that I would likely be caught and killed if I tried to go there.
Not waiting for an answer, they stalked out.

I told Marcel my dilemma as soon as he arrived next morning.
He went straight to Theobald, who was still in charge of worker
welfare at Cimerwa.

Theobald suggested I write a letter to the three directors,
requesting that my children and I be allowed to remain in the clinic.
Before delivering my letter, Theobald added his own comment:
"Applicant still belongs to our company. We should favorably
consider her request."

However, the directors' reply insisted, "Applicant must immediately vacate health center. She may resume residence in her
previous home."

I saw through this trick. The gate and doors of my previous
home had been destroyed. The directors knew my sons and I would

not last long there. Interahamwe would make short work of us, and the three of them would be conveniently rid of us, without dirtying their own hands with our deaths.

Thankfully, Theobald was also responsible for construction and maintenance of company buildings. When he learned of the directors' reply, he sent workers to repair my house.

On the appointed date, I wrapped my children's few clothes into a bundle. Fortunately for me, Interahamwe had moved off to other regions, though I shrank from imagining where they were and what they were doing. The Cimerwa guard scanned the area. When there was no one around, he opened the gate – and we walked out. Our interval of asylum in Cimerwa's health center was over.

My faithful friend Faina had just arrived, with cassava and beans to share from her own meager supply. I asked her to walk with me. She carried Petit and our clothes, as well as the food. I carried Christian, so we could quickly cover the short distance. Charles-Vital walked at my side.

Celestin accompanied us too, as he had on the day we had come to the clinic. Looking grave, he cautioned me to keep my front gate locked at all times. I needed no such warning; I knew I would double-check the lock every day.

And so we returned to our apartment, scene of such conflicting memories. When we arrived, Faina transferred the baby to my back and hurried off for more supplies. I unlocked the door.

As soon as I stepped in, I backed quickly out again. I'd known the place had been ransacked, but I was not prepared for the shambles of crumpled papers and broken dishes scattered across the floor. And the smell . . . But we needed shelter. So, taking a deep breath, I walked in.

Anything of any value had disappeared – refrigerator, sideboard, table, chairs, sofa . . . Gone were our traditional carvings and statuary, the milk-and-butter gourd (a symbol of prosperity that every bride receives at her wedding) chinaware, vases, the artwork that had brightened our walls – all the touches of beauty I had brought in, everything that had made this house our home. Even the windows had been stripped of their curtains.

Overcome, I slumped to the floor. It wasn't the possessions I grieved for, it was what they represented: my husband, our love for each other, the life we had built together. What hurt most was the betrayal – my own neighbors wantonly destroying our life.

Petit protested on my back, prompting me to pull myself together, for his and his brothers' sake. Standing up, I continued to make my way through the apartment. It took all my courage to even look into my bedroom, where the dark stains on floor and walls screamed at me. But I had to enter, to learn if I had anything left.

Bed, mattress, blankets, clothing, leather purse – my engagement gift from Charles – bassinet, radio, wedding chest, jewelry, and books were gone. Here, too, papers strewed the floor. Collecting them up, I realized all my documents were missing, as were pictures of my relatives. Interahamwe used their victims' photos, I had heard, to identify further targets.

Mechanically, I started sorting through the rubbish – until I felt something my fingers recognized immediately: my precious journal. Finding it seemed a glimmer of God's love, a sign that he still cared. Carefully, I pulled this treasure from the trash.

Torn and dirty, the small book was open; stamped across its spread was the messy print of a shoe – a footprint in dried blood. Overcome, I closed the journal and hugged it to my chest. The blood of my loved ones, now preserved forever, made sacred this connection to the past, this record of our family struggles and sorrow.

Looking up, I was again overwhelmed by what had happened in this room. The stench was nauseating – and far worse than the odor was what it signified. I knew I could never sleep here again. Journal in hand, I firmly closed the bedroom door behind me.

Faina was just returning with clean clothes. Dear Faina! She will never know how much she taught me. She did not measure people by rank or wealth; she helped me when I had everything and when I was destitute.

Now I, too, was starting to realize that valuing possessions is pointless. What good had mine done? They had only invited envy. Life alone is precious. Love alone has value. So when Faina gave me some of her own *kitenges* to replace my missing clothes, I wasn't troubled that they were of poor quality cotton.

Other Hutu came to my aid. Theobald and a coworker, Mathias, brought two metal beds and some quilts from the Chinese employees' abandoned quarters. Another former colleague brought mattresses. A neighbor, Josiane, had her houseboy bring food, not only on our arrival but regularly through the following weeks. I was thankful, because of course I could not leave the house, and my last sacks of rice, beans, and sugar had vanished, along with all the pots, pans, and utensils from my kitchen hut.

I decided my children and I would sleep in the guest room, where the smell was bearable and where haunting images would not stare at me from behind the door. Petit cried through the whole first night, sensing, I'm sure, the evil that had intruded here. I could not console him, and I worried that his crying would attract Interahamwe.

I felt like crying too. Here I was, alone with three children in this desolate place. Only Hutu surrounded us – most openly hostile, others shunning me in fear of what Interahamwe might do to them. I was an outsider. Or maybe I was their guilty conscience, my presence an unwelcome reminder of why the other Tutsi were absent.

But I still had my three sons. In each, I saw something of their father. This both pained and comforted me. They were my only reason to go on living, and they did more for me than they will ever understand – Charles-Vital and Christian with their childish ways and words, Petit with his trust and wide smiles. His big brothers knew how to get a response from him – tickling, making faces, and surprising him into gales of giggles.

Still, I could not smile. I was certain I would never sing or laugh again. I felt as broken and empty as my plundered house, as cold as the inside of my stolen fridge. *How would I manage to keep my children safe?* I wondered wearily. *Would they ever know normal life?*

Dejected though I was, I started writing in my journal again.

One afternoon, Josiane's two daughters came over to play. They joined Charles-Vital and Christian, building miniature houses with stones and twigs in the backyard. Next day they came again. It was a relief to hear them laughing and shouting with my children as they all kicked and chased a ball made from banana leaves.

My respite was broken, however, by an urgent summons from the front gate. It was Josiane's husband. When I opened, he barged through my house to where his children were playing out back.

Shaking his older child, he rebuked her harshly: "Don't you *dare* come here again!"

Then he grabbed the younger one by the hand and marched them both away. At the gate he turned, calmer now.

"I have nothing against you, Denise," he said. "But Interahamwe might kill my girls if they're seen with Tutsi kids."

My heart was heavy. I didn't want my sons burdened with my sorrow. I didn't want them to share my emptiness. And I didn't want them to absorb the prejudice that filled our world.

The little radio Louitpold had brought to the clinic remained my link to the world. I kept its volume turned low and hid it under my mattress. From the BBC I learned the news, both good and bad. I heard that the RPF had liberated most of the country, although our southwest tip was still furthest from their reach. I also learned that France was planning to send "humanitarian support" to Rwanda. I knew the French had worked closely with extremist Hutu for decades, so I mistrusted their motives and feared that their coming boded ill for us surviving Tutsi.

Sure enough, the radio soon reported that the French battalion had been welcomed by jubilant Interahamwe waving French flags, flowers, and machetes. Our peril persisted.

Jonas was a Cimerwa worker Charles and I had known. He was Hutu, but both his mother and his wife were Tutsi. One day he appeared at my gate. He had just smuggled his Tutsi mother-in-law to the Congo, and he now offered to do the same for me and my children. "Be ready in three days," he said.

When Jonas returned three days later, however, he said, "I had a dream last night, and I don't know what it means. I saw myself and many other Hutu fleeing toward the Congo. We were rushing, and we were carrying our possessions. We had become very thirsty. In the middle of the forest, we came upon a spring of water – and you were sitting beside it, Denise! We all threw down our bundles to drink from the pool."

"*Where* was this spring?" I questioned Jonas. "Was it on the Rwandan side of the border, or had you crossed into the Congo?" His answer was important to me.

"The spring of fresh water was in Rwanda," Jonas replied.

"That means I am meant to stay here," I told him firmly. "I cannot flee to the Congo now."

Jonas agreed with my interpretation, and we took leave of each other.

I continued to ponder the dream's message. I had a growing sense that God would someday rebuild Rwanda, making it a spring of peace and justice – yes, even of love.

FROM THEIR HANGOUT at Casimir's Musikiti Bar opposite my house, Hutu militia sent a message that they were aware I had moved home and would soon come after me and my children. They seemed to enjoy biding their time, like lions or leopards playing with a mouse.

Knowing they targeted males doubled my fear. I discussed my concern with Celestin, who dropped in regularly to check on me. He visited my neighbor, asking to borrow her daughters' dresses for my boys. She gave him two, and I felt a little more at ease seeing

Charles-Vital and Christian playing in the backyard dressed as girls – until the militia sent a second message, informing me that they were not deceived.

They insinuated further dark hints. Did I know, they called across the road, that everyone at Kamarampaka Stadium – including my companions from the clinic – had been moved to Nyarushishi Refugee Camp? There were ten thousand Tutsi there now, conveniently collected for . . . They left the sentence hanging, knowing my imagination could complete it.

My mind was screaming.

Where is the rest of the world in all this? Surely other countries must know what is happening in Rwanda. Why aren't they intervening, to prevent endless bloodshed? Don't people care that ten thousand more Tutsi are about to be butchered?

June 25 was a Saturday. Around nine o'clock that morning, pandemonium drew me to the front window. Looking cautiously out, I saw Interahamwe rushing toward the cement plant. Yussuf Munyakazi was among them, calling to the company sentry that they needed all Cimerwa's big trucks – fast.

They had to drive to Nyarushishi Refugee Camp immediately, he shouted. The government had ordered them to kill everyone there today, before the RPF got any closer.

Helplessly I watched militants hustling to bring weapons, open garage doors, back out vehicles. Cimerwa's three directors were with them, supporting every move. I left the window – there were no curtains to hide me – but I heard everything: voices yelling, truck horns blaring, engines revving, and, above the motors, Interahamwe roaring their conquest song as they drove off, *Yego mubatsembe tsembe!* "Yes, we will exterminate them!"

Accustomed to chaos, Christian and Charles-Vital played blithely out back, while Petit slept peacefully on my bed. But I was beside myself. I pictured the unsuspecting victims in Nyarushishi

Camp: Goretti with Kim, Diane, and the new baby, the others I had been with in the health center – and ten thousand more.

I collapsed to my knees. As a child, I had wondered what the Bible meant when it described Jacob wrestling with the Lord. Now I myself battled for the lives of ten thousand Tutsi in Nyarushishi. I railed at God.

How can you allow this slaughter, after protecting these people through two terrible months? Are you really a gracious and merciful God? Or do you care only for Hutu? How do I know you even exist? This is your last chance. If the enemy's plan is foiled, then I will believe in you!

Never before had I defied the Almighty like this. But I did not feel his wrath. I did not feel anything that proved he was real. Exhausted, I lay down beside Petit. I wanted to weep, but my tears had burned up, my heart was scorched dry.

Six hours later I heard a distant, growing rumble. The sound became unmistakable: Cimerwa's trucks. Peering out, I saw the morning's convoy returning. What had happened? They could not have fulfilled their cruel mission so quickly; they had barely had time to get to Nyarushishi and back. I heard angry shouts as the Cimerwa trucks were parked.

Many years later, I learned that when Yussuf Munyakazi and his Interahamwe arrived at Nyarushishi to kill everyone in the camp, a Rwandan military officer had intercepted them. Orders had changed, he told them. The French had warned the Rwandans that the international community was aware of Nyarushishi Camp. There could be very awkward questions to answer if its inhabitants disappeared.

THE NEXT EVENING, after tucking Charles-Vital and Christian into bed, I unlocked the front gate. Annemarie and Saidi were still paying Charlotte to help me with shopping and housework. She had spent the weekend with her parents, but I expected her back any moment. Petit was awake, so I held him in the crook of one arm and tidied the apartment with the other while awaiting my housegirl's return.

Hearing a slight sound, I looked up – and froze. Instead of Charlotte, a big man filled the doorway, a blade at his side and grenades dangling from his belt. My mouth went dry. I knew him: Harorimana. It was he who had supervised Manasseh's execution. Without a word, he strode in and stood before me.

Fear almost paralyzed me, but I managed to stammer, "What do you want?"

Beating his chest, he smirked, "I will protect you!"

In one swift, sudden action, Harorimana swept Petit from my arm and raised him high. My baby, utterly unafraid, opened his mouth in his wide, trusting smile.

Harorimana grinned, exclaiming, *Igisekeramwanzi!* "The smile of one who laughs in his enemy's face!"

Terror spread from my throat to my chest and right to my fingertips. I didn't dare move or speak. I had heard too many accounts of what Interahamwe did to baby boys . . .

At this moment Celestin and Marcel, returning from the Sunday evening service, noticed my open gate – not a good sign – so turned into my front yard and walked up to the house. Grasping the situation at a glance, they started a casual conversation.

"Good evening, Harorimana, how are you?" inquired Celestin.

"I'm fine, thanks," he replied. "I've come to visit Denise. What about you?"

"Oh, we're just dropping by," answered Marcel. "We're on our way home from church and thought we'd see how Denise is doing."

"Well, it's good to see you," Harorimana said, embarrassed. "I think I'll get us all something to drink."

Passing me the baby, he hurried out the front door and gate. We three watched in silence as he crossed the road and bought some Fanta at the Musikiti Bar.

Returning, he set the bottle on the table, then said abruptly, "Well, goodnight everyone!" and walked out.

My knees gave way, and I sat down fast.

"Are you out of your mind, Denise?" Celestin chided. "Harori-mana would have raped you! He's been telling everyone he's going to make you his 'wife.' For goodness sake, keep your gate locked, like I told you!"

Still trembling, I promised, and they left.

After locking gate and door, I dropped to my knees, thanking God for these two brothers who had saved both my honor and my child's life.

II

Survivors

IN JULY, realizing their defeat was near, the extremist Hutu
government fled Kigali and moved to our southwestern region.
The Rwandan army pitched camp beside our cement plant. These
government troops were noticeably more agitated each day, until
their last semblance of discipline crumbled. Through my window,
I saw the soldiers ransack the factory, along with Cimerwa
employees, Interahamwe, and police.

Fear filled Bugarama. RTLM, the station everyone still tuned
to, was shrieking that the RPF would certainly carry out recrimi-
nations to avenge the genocide. My Hutu neighbors were paranoid.
And survivors like me were fearful that Interahamwe would
eliminate the last Tutsi witnesses before taking flight. I knew my
children and I would have been dead many times over, had it not
been for my few Hutu friends watching out for us.

Celestin called on a small group of Christians to fast and pray. I
was too fatigued to fast, but I prayed without ceasing.

On July 4 the RPF took control of Kigali, and on July 18 they declared a cease-fire. The war and genocide were over, they announced over the radio, and a new government of unity and reconciliation would be established. They named Pasteur Bizimungu as our new president and Paul Kagame as vice president.

Despite the new government's assurances of peace, most Hutu were still convinced that reprisals would follow. Cimerwa's management assembled the employees to announce that the factory was closed. Workers would receive their wages one last time; then they were free to leave "before the rebels arrive."

A mass exodus began. Guilty and innocent alike were fleeing before imagined retribution.

Celestin dropped by my house. He believed life would become increasingly dangerous in our corner of Rwanda – a pipeline for fleeing Hutu – and he suggested my family move to the building where our prayer group met. I took his advice. On the way, my boys and I were overtaken by Hutu on the run, dragging mattresses, suitcases, and mats, or balancing dishes and luggage on their heads, hurrying toward the Congo.

Arriving at the house of prayer, I discovered that others had had the same idea. We were quite a group. As evening darkened, however, the building felt unsafe to me; I had heard of too many church massacres. The other people also seemed anxious, and most of us moved into a nearby banana plantation. We heard shots, and I could not rest.

Petit cried most of the night. The people hiding with us were afraid we would be discovered because of my baby's crying. But I guess everyone else was too busy pillaging – or running – to bother with us.

Next morning Celestin found my boys and me in the banana grove. I told him I did not want to return to the prayer building. He said returning to my house was not an option either; two soldiers had been there, looking for me. So he and his wife invited us to stay with them. Thérèse became like a sister to me in the following days. She let my children sleep with theirs and gladly provided us all with food. I helped with household chores.

From Thérèse and Celestin's house, I had a clear view of what was happening at the factory. It was mayhem; looting seemed to give people superhuman strength. I watched one man haul out an enormous cupboard and run off with it. Another emerged carrying a desk on his head.

Around this time I came across the words of the prophet Jeremiah, "If you stay in this land, I will build you up and not tear you down; I will plant you and not uproot you, for I have relented concerning the disaster I have inflicted on you." But although I believed God wanted me in Rwanda, I was now homeless here. So, after prayer and discussion with my hosts, I decided to try to reconnect with my parents in the Congo. We had managed to communicate in recent weeks through a visiting teacher, so I knew they were in Bwegera.

Theobald was still in Bugarama. Before departing, I found him and asked the company's permission to visit my parents. He signed a paper, allowing an official leave of absence. This was important to me: I was not fleeing.

My sons and I left from Bugarama for Bwegera on Monday, August 8. An acquaintance, Abdul, drove us all the way. In normal times, I might have considered this God's idea of a joke. Even in my stress, its irony reached me: Abdul was Yussuf Munyakazi's nephew.

A year or two earlier, Yussuf had planned to murder Abdul – who defied his views – but the young man caught wind of the plot and left the country until the old regime toppled. Now he had returned to Bugarama for cement. His arrival was a godsend, because public transport had broken down – and joining fleeing Interahamwe on foot was out of the question.

When I chanced to meet Abdul at Cimerwa's gate, he was startled to see me alive. He agreed immediately when I asked if he would give my children and me a ride to Bwegera, and within an hour we were off.

He drove carefully, as we passed thousands of Hutu pedestrians fleeing along the road.

"How did your Uncle Yussuf become such a villain?" I asked. "He was not always so cruel. Charles and I even traveled to a wedding with him once, singing and laughing all the way."

"I know exactly when he changed," Abdul replied. "Three years ago, he was invited to a get-together with high-up government and military brass. The president himself was in that meeting. I don't know what they discussed, but I can guess. Uncle Yussuf felt flattered that he, a farmer, was consulted by bigwigs. That was the day he sold his soul."

We drove on in silence, as I brooded and Abdul focused on the road. But as we swung around a corner, he slammed on the brakes. I gasped, gripping Petit so tightly, he cried out. Blocking our way was a barricade of planks. And behind it, belligerent and bold – as if they still ruled Rwanda – a row of Interahamwe held their positions, machetes in hand.

Oh God! Have we been spared all these weeks only to be hacked up now?

Abdul, however, seemed unfazed. Lazily rolling down his window, he stared into the eyes of the leader – whose flicker of recognition betrayed that he knew his commander's nephew. Without a word, Abdul handed over a roll of money, which vanished into the man's pocket.

A quick gesture, and the planks were removed. We were on our way.

I did not relax again.

The Congolese barrier, too, opened like magic when Abdul slipped some money to the border guard. Silently I thanked God for sending this angel – never mind that he was kin to my archenemy.

In Bwegera at last, it was overwhelming to reunite with my parents and three youngest siblings, who could hardly believe we were alive. What a relief to pass my boys into their grandparents' embrace.

"Denise," my mother wept, "I was praying, praying! Always, I pictured you alone and sorrowful, without your husband."

We all grieved that evening, for those who were dead and those who were missing. I still had no word of Charles.

The next morning, with a jolt, I realized our continuing danger. When I went to the market, whom should I meet but Bugarama's former mayor – the one who had read out the names of those destined for Kamarampaka Stadium. He gave me a cold stare.

"Yes, Denise," Papa sighed when I told him, "this part of the Congo is swarming with Interahamwe and their collaborators."

My parents and I talked, while my brother Ntampaka and two sisters occupied my children in the back room. Since there was obviously no safety here, where I was a known witness to Hutu crimes, we quickly made our decision: we would go to Burundi to pick up any other family members wanting to join us, then travel to some area of Rwanda that was fully liberated – unlike Bugarama in the border triangle, where the situation was so precarious.

During the following days, I recognized more killers in the marketplace, so I started staying closer to home and kept my children with me. It was a relief when our family finally left for Burundi on August 26, walking east to the Ruzizi River with many other Tutsi who shared our anxiety. Congolese government soldiers accompanied our band to the border, to protect us from renegade Interahamwe.

Before departing, I left word with Bwegera neighbors – to ease my husband's search, if he should come looking for us.

Crossing the Ruzizi on the ferry brought back my childhood journey, when our family had crossed in the opposite direction, moving from Burundi to the Congo. At age seven, I had mistrusted the river's murky depths, recalling tales of hippopotamuses that could capsize boats and crocodiles that could devour people in seconds. I had planted myself on the bank, while Papa patiently explained that our craft was too big to be bothered by creatures. I had finally taken his word for it, but my eyes probed the muddy water throughout our crossing. After scrambling ashore on the Congo side, I sprinted up the bank before anything nasty could emerge from the mud to grab and eat me.

That seemed an eternity ago. If only my own children could be so naïve, I thought – if only underwater animals were their greatest fear! I felt like weeping for my sons, who would never know a care-free childhood.

Once over the river, we caught public transport for the final stretch through Burundi. Three of my adult brothers – Phocas, Jean de Dieu, and Steven – welcomed us in Bujumbura. But they were shocked at my appearance. Due to stress, meager diet, and stomach trouble, I had lost twenty-five pounds; my skin was peeling, and my hair was infested with lice. My brothers would see thousands like me in the next months.

My extended family showed great kindness to my children and me. My sister Rose bought us all clothes, and Phocas got me a new radio so I could listen to soothing music.

After some discussion among the adults, most of us decided to relocate to Kigali. We rented a bus, with other returnees, and set off on August 30. Once more, I left word of my whereabouts, in case Charles should turn up.

We found ourselves joining a human river. Thousands of expatriate Tutsi had made the same decision to return to Rwanda, now freed from the government that had exiled them. There was no hearty homecoming camaraderie among us, however. Each person, occupied with private worries, seemed a tense mix of hope and dread. After crossing into Rwanda, we were further sobered at the sight of burned, roofless huts throughout the countryside.

As we passed through Butare, I pressed my face to the window, longing to see an uncle who had lived in this town. It was just possible that Eli had survived, I thought, since he had not lived near Tateh Ephraim and Tateh Damaris like the rest of his family.

Suddenly I glimpsed someone beside the street who looked like him – only much older . . .

"Stop the bus!" I shouted, grabbing my father's arm. "It's Uncle Eli!" The driver braked, and we almost fell out of the vehicle in our haste.

My father called. Uncle Eli looked up. For a moment he stood still, staring. Then, running into each other's arms, the brothers embraced. Tears coursed down their cheeks as they remembered their parents and each of their brothers and sisters – a large family, now reduced to these two.

Uncle Eli said his sons had also been killed; both had hidden with a Methodist pastor, but someone had betrayed them.

Papa wrote down Uncle Eli's address, then we were on our way once more.

Phocas had friends who found us a room in their apartment building. We were thankful for shelter, but we knew we couldn't stay long; we were eleven people.

Next morning, my mother looked after the children so my brothers and I could seek more permanent lodgings. A young RPF soldier offered to show us a range of unoccupied houses. There were many after the genocide. Walking the streets, we could not avoid the sight of decaying bodies under bushes and beside the road.

Twelve-year-old Ntampaka kept exclaiming, "Dead four months, and not buried?"

Every house was worse than the last. In one, we opened the door to a cloud of flies swarming over a putrefying corpse. Horror engulfed me. I couldn't stand the sight and smell of one more dead body. In each I saw my husband, who might be lying somewhere like this.

We finally reached an affluent neighborhood and approached a yellow bungalow. Our guide recommended this property as hardly damaged. Its lawns and shrubs seemed inviting, and a eucalyptus grove spread up a grassy slope behind the house.

Walking in, we began to explore. The dining room looked attractive, though stripped of furniture. I stepped into the next room – and gagged. One glimpse of the blood-soaked carpet sent me running outdoors, my heart pounding.

I couldn't take any more. I had to get back to my children and my mother.

My brothers house-hunted without me after this – but I insisted that I could not live where someone had been murdered. They finally found a compound vacated by Hutu fleeing the liberation army. We settled in, with the few belongings we had brought. I had my own room, and my boys had theirs.

My father quickly found a job, since there was a severe shortage of medical personnel in the capital. At Kigali Hospital, he heard tragic reports from coworkers and patients alike. He often brought orphans home, some of whom stayed several weeks. We shared what we had, and they recounted their experiences.

One boy told us, "When Interahamwe attacked, I ran into the Catholic church with other Tutsi. My sister said it would be safe, but the killers followed us. I jumped out a window, into a back-yard. There was a kennel, so I crawled in. The big watchdog didn't stop me, didn't even bark or growl. He let me share the food and water that a nun brought him every day. She never noticed me behind the dog, although I stayed many days and nights. That dog is my best friend."

Mama lived up to her nickname, Karibu Kwangu, making everyone welcome. More than once, someone asked me, "Denise, why aren't you like your mother? She is always serving, singing, reaching out. You're like an ice cube!"

I didn't know how to answer. I envied my parents and my siblings, who had been elsewhere during the genocide. They saw its results, and they certainly grieved for the dead; our father's family had been killed, our mother's family had been killed, dear friends had been killed, and old neighbors had been killed. But my parents, brothers, and sisters would never know the smell of fear, the terror of the slaughter – or my ongoing inner struggle.

Often I could not even think clearly. Once, on the street, I met a Tutsi girl I recognized from Bugarama. She and I stared at each other without a word or nod of greeting, before walking off in opposite directions. We had both seen too much death to comprehend that the other could still be alive.

Since early April, I had been under siege or on the go, with no time to relax or to think beyond my children's immediate safety. Now that life settled into a semblance of routine, my mind kicked into gear, and thoughts churned like a cement mixer, keeping me awake for hours every night.

I wrestled with the fact that I had survived when most Tutsi had not. I was no better than the others – yet I was alive, and they were dead.

Guilt stalked me. I remembered my houseful of people on April 16. Now Anselm, Manasseh, Thérèse, Aline, and Epa were dead. I recalled leaping into the bathroom with my toddler, locking the door against danger – but innocent people had been locked out as well. If I had pushed Aline or Thérèse ahead of me, might they still be alive?

And then Thérèse's moans would haunt me. She had died alone, praying for help, while I hid a few feet away . . . Where could I flee from memories like these?

Often, I wished I had died with the others. But then my spirit would rise up: *No! My children need me! I must live, so they can too.*

I grieved that my sons had witnessed murder, fearing that this had permanently affected their souls. Their entire generation was damaged; over ninety percent of Rwanda's children had watched people being killed.

Tutsi children were burdened with fear. Hutu children were burdened with guilt. Both carried tremendous confusion. Unnumbered youngsters had no male role model. Tutsi fathers were dead, and Hutu fathers were gone too, because the new government was arresting thousands of perpetrators, whose wives would now have to raise families alone. These women became known as prison widows, a term I deeply resented. They knew where their husbands were. They could visit them.

Although I believed in God, I had only accusing questions to bring before him. "You could have prevented all this!" I cried, again and again. "Why didn't you?"

Another question tormented me. The Hutu had been in power, and they had killed us – but what if we Tutsi had been in control? What if *we* had been the majority? Would we have killed the Hutu? Could *I* be like that?

My husband's unknown fate plagued my dreams. *Oh Charles, what did they do to you? What did you suffer? Where did they put you?*

If he was dead, how had he died? Tortured? Beheaded? I hated these thoughts, but they had become an out-of-control truck careening off the road. I remembered my aunt and uncle and their seven children who had drowned in Lake Kivu. I could almost envy them.

I knew this interlude with my parents would not last forever, but I hoped it could give me some measure of peace and strength to face the future. Every night the extended family met for prayer. It was painfully different from our childhood, however, when I had sung, prayed, and listened to Papa's Bible stories with a child's trust that God had everything in hand. Life had been so simple back then. Now horrible sounds and images replayed through my brain.

Alone, I pored over my Bible, desperately longing for God's nearness. But when I tried to focus on the future, I sensed only dense darkness blocking my way like suffocating smog. Often, all I could do was pray to Jesus, hoping he would understand since he, too, had been hated, betrayed, and humiliated. Clinging to his cross was like clinging to the trunk of a palm through a hurricane. I might be battered by lashing wind, but surely the tree's roots would hold.

A young evangelist, Innocent, lived on the opposite side of our courtyard. Every morning he stood at his open window singing, "Praise the Lord, O my soul. All my inmost being, praise his holy name." His morning ritual, waking me from troubled sleep, was a balm pouring over my wounded spirit.

October 5 was Christian's second birthday. Since we were now safe, surrounded by my caring family, I decided to try to make the day special. Forcing some cheer into my voice, I woke my second son. Christian opened his eyes, looked into mine, and said, "My papa – is he dead?"

My child's question shook me. I decided it was time to try to find out what had happened to Charles. Until now, I had clung to the slim chance of his swimming to safety. And I think I had hoped that, if I didn't press, good news might drop into my ears from some passerby. Whenever I walked through the city, even with my mind on other matters, I subconsciously checked every side street, my ears alert for my husband's voice and my eyes scanning the throng for his face, his posture, his gait. But time was moving on, and hope dimmed with each evening.

The day after Christian's birthday, I went downtown, determined to inquire. It was difficult to know how to start such a search. But people had come to Kigali from every corner of Rwanda, so I started asking anyone from the area where Charles had been working. Most knew nothing.

One person said, "He must have been killed that first day."

Another thought he might have fled to the Congo – which got me hoping again.

Although I learned nothing of Charles, I discovered that his mother, Consoletia, was here in Kigali, just half a mile from us. After the cease-fire, staff of the United Nations High Commissioner for Refugees had found her in critical condition in Nyarushishi Refugee Camp. UNHCR sent her to Kigali for treatment, accompanied by a surviving daughter, Emerance. On Consoletia's release from Kigali Hospital, Emerance chanced to see and recognize my father. Papa told me immediately, and I managed to find the small room the two of them shared.

When I found Consoletia, I had to tell her that her son Anselm had been murdered in my house, on April 16, and that I did not know what had happened to Charles. She was already sinking in despair, and my words pushed her deeper. Her husband and most of their eleven children were dead. She was too depressed to talk, and I did not stay long.

Trudging back from this painful reunion, I recalled the first time I'd met Consoletia, before Charles and I were married. I had loved visiting Mukoma back then, and he and I made the ninety-minute drive from Bugarama as often as we could. When not shrouded in mist, the hilltop had a spectacular view of Lake Kivu.

The clouds were dumping rain, however, the first morning he brought me to his childhood home, and our Cimerwa car had swerved through deep mud on the last hill. Finally abandoning the vehicle, we had slogged the last stretch on foot.

Arriving spattered with rust-colored mud did nothing to alleviate my nervousness at meeting my future in-laws, but Consoletia had quickly put me at ease. Laughing, she had shown me where to wash and asked me to help her. She and her husband hosted visitors nearly every day, she explained; their compound was the largest in Mukoma. With so many guests, children, and grandchildren, Consoletia was busy from dawn to dusk, and she welcomed my help.

While she and I chopped onions and vegetables that day, Consoletia had described her childhood and youth in nearby Shangi, where she had been born in 1926, during the reign of Rwanda's King Musinga. The population was expected to supply the king's household back then, and she had helped other children bring fruit and vegetables to his servants. She recalled seeing white men for the first time when she was seven, and being shocked by their pale faces.

One of the first to be baptized at Shangi Catholic Mission, Consoletia had married Callixte Kayumba there in 1942 – a teenage bride – and then moved to his home in Mukoma.

In 1959, a wave of anti-Tutsi violence had forced them to flee, and they escaped by boat to Idjwi Island with the six sons and daughters they had by then. Refugee life was stressful, and they had returned to Rwanda some months later, as soon as her husband believed it would be safe. That's when distinctions were made between Hutu and Tutsi in Mukoma's school, and Charles and his siblings had been mistreated by their classmates.

Even with top grades, almost no Tutsi student could pursue further education. This had been a disappointment to Callixte and Consoletia, who had hoped their children would enjoy better opportunities than their own. Four of their sons eventually attended university in the Congo, becoming geologist, engineer, agriculturalist, and priest before returning to support the family in Rwanda.

My parents, too, had liked Callixte and Consoletia from the start. When they first met, the two mothers discovered how much they had in common. Both had spent their childhoods tending cows within sight of Lake Kivu, and neither had ever attended school, yet they both had lively minds and were eager to learn about the wider world. They couldn't stop talking when they got together, and they'd had great fun planning our wedding.

I shook my head in sorrow at these memories. Having known Consoletia's vibrant personality, it was doubly difficult to find this empty shell of the woman I knew. Our Kigali encounter left me so disheartened, I almost wished we had not met. But at least she now knew she had three living grandsons – and me. In my heart, I vowed to be faithful to her as Ruth, in the Bible, had been to her mother-in-law Naomi.

Consoletia did not stay in Kigali. She soon returned to Mukoma, and it would be a couple of years before I saw her again. I could not have imagined, in 1994, how our relationship would blossom into something beautiful again in the future, when my mother-in-law – healed from her misery – would radiate even more love and joy than she had in the past.

One day I heard that Cimerwa's Kigali office was resuming business. On paper, I was still employed by Cimerwa. I went to inquire and was surprised to meet Theobald, who explained that he had been made general director of both branches of the company.

When I asked about a job, he said, "We don't need you here in Kigali, but we do in Bugarama, because so many workers there fled to the Congo. You could start work there immediately."

I promised to think it over. But I insisted that if I returned to Bugarama, I could not live in my previous home. It held too many difficult memories.

"No problem," Theobald replied. "There are lots of empty houses. I'm sure we can find something."

I knew I could trust this director, who had kept his promises and helped me in the past. He seemed so approachable now, I found courage to ask, "Can Cimerwa lend me some money? I'll repay it from my future salary."

"You don't need to borrow," he answered. "You lost everything, through no fault of your own. On the company's behalf, here are 40,000 francs."

I accepted the money thankfully. On the way back to my parents' place, I bought a mattress for my children, my heart a little lighter for one man's kindness.

It was in Kigali, too, that I was reunited with Goretti. I happened to glance out, one October afternoon, to see her turn into our compound. Her colorful *kitenge* caught my eye, and I immediately recognized my dearest neighbor. The same instant, I knew something was wrong. She should have had a baby on her back.

It was half a year since I had watched the Kamarampaka-bound truck carry Goretti and the others away from our refuge in Cimerwa's health center. Now I hurried out to meet her, and we embraced at the door. But I felt no surge of warmth or joy. How can I explain this? We were best friends, we had thought each other dead – yet we could neither laugh nor cry at this reunion.

We looked into each other's expressionless eyes for several moments before Goretti spoke. She had learned of my presence from Theobald – she too had gone to Cimerwa's Kigali office looking for work – and had come straightaway to find me.

She now told me she believed her baby had died on April 16, when the killers struck her, because she had felt no internal movement during her stay in Cimerwa's clinic. At her words, pictures sprang to mind from the start of the year: the two of us chatting across the fence between our yards, sharing our expectancy, or sewing and knitting in her house or mine, getting everything ready for our little ones. Now my Petit was six months old, and Goretti's child was dead.

"A couple days after we reached the stadium, a priest visiting from Cyangugu told the Red Cross to take me to the hospital, where a doctor gave me an injection to induce labor. The next day, May 2, my baby was stillborn, a perfect little boy. He looked like he was sleeping. The people at the hospital gave him to me, so I had time to see and hold him." Goretti's mechanical-sounding voice conveyed nothing of her anguish at losing this long-awaited child, so soon after her eldest son, who had been sadistically killed before her eyes.

A Hutu businessman had driven Goretti back to Kamarampaka Stadium to rejoin her eleven-year-old daughter and twelve-year-old son. Neither had had anything to eat during her absence, and Diane's wounds had become infected.

"A few days later, my husband Viateur's relatives appeared from Bukavu, in the Congo, and found us," Goretti continued. "They took us, and we stayed with them, while Kim, Diane, and I recovered. Now, when I arrived here in Kigali, I learned that all my brothers were killed. Some of my sisters are alive, but three of them lost their husbands, and most of their children are dead."

As Goretti and I parted, we agreed to keep in touch. But again, there was no emotion in our words.

She and I were not the only ones who seemed disoriented. Wherever I walked, I saw people with eyes as vacant as my own. We all seemed under a spell, unable to comprehend what had happened.

We never would comprehend it.

12

Peace with Bugarama

MY PARENTS OPPOSED the idea of my returning to Bugarama, offering to help me find alternate employment in Kigali. I debated with myself. I felt no desire to return to the site of my ordeal; but I had come to believe, during my last difficult weeks there, that God had a task for me in Bugarama.

In early November, I made my decision: my children and I would move back to the factory town.

I set out with trepidation. After our three-month absence, how would I meet – and live with – people who had killed my friends and cousins, who had called my sons snakes and insects, who had planned our death?

And what about those who had not wielded machetes but had howled, "Kill them! Kill them!" – and then snuck into my house to riffle through my belongings, taking whatever suited them? Whom could I trust?

Thérèse and Celestin welcomed us back into their home, even though they could not fathom why I would return. A few days later, Cimerwa gave me a house, as Theobald had promised. Moving in took no time, as I possessed only what I had carried. I could hardly remember what it was like to own a houseful of useful belongings and objects of beauty.

I felt a stifling atmosphere throughout town, as if a curse lay over Bugarama's vast factory buildings and housing development. Every day, on the street, I met Hutu who had killed my people or trashed my home. They averted their eyes when we passed. Apprehension weighed me down as I walked the familiar roads, and I panicked if I saw someone carrying a machete, on his way to work his fields.

My fridge had been installed in a store downtown, and Josephine told me which homes held my table and chairs, my beds, my baby bassinet. She urged me to claim my furniture, but I was not tempted. The thieves were accomplices to murder; anything they had used would be tainted with blood.

When I hiked out to our allotment, I discovered that all my cassava, corn, potatoes, and beans had been ripped from the ground. As I started replanting my desolate plot, hurt and angry, I sensed that people were watching from a distance.

The minister of my church had fled to the Congo along with the killers. The new minister made forgiveness the theme of his sermons, directing his preaching at Tutsi survivors. This enraged me. I thought pastors like him, who had been directly or indirectly involved in murder, should begin by humbling themselves. That never happened. I resented him, and all the Hutu Christians who had looked the other way during my trials. Even now, very few from church visited my home, although they all knew I was back.

I begged God to help me respond to their duplicity – and overcome my resentment. My prayers seemed to go nowhere. I was so frustrated with myself, as well as with my neighbors, that forgiving seemed impossible. It was just too high a hurdle for me to leap.

As my bitterness festered, I decided to fast. Every Tuesday, I ate nothing and redoubled my prayers. Pouring out my torment and challenging God with my questions, I felt like an animal caught in a net, my inner thrashing only entangling me further.

Why did you let over a million Tutsi be killed? And what about the survivors, now scarred and destitute? Don't you care about the children with no parents? How will our battered people start families again? And how am I supposed to carry on, surrounded by these hypocrites?

My conflict came to a climax one morning when I met a woman, on the street outside my house, wearing my best dress. It was precious to me – though I had never even worn it. Charles had helped me choose the bright fabric, and a friend in Burundi had sewn the *kitenge* for me to wear after my baby's birth. Across my memory flashed my husband's face, radiating pleasure, as he handed me the colorful cloth.

Hatred and fury boiled within me as the woman sashayed by. Darting indoors, and into my bedroom, I slammed the door and fell to my knees.

"Oh God, why did you send me back here?" I raged. "How can I live with these fiends, these devils, these killers?"

And then God answered – as clearly as if I'd heard him with my ears: "Denise, give these people a chance to know who I am, so they can repent. I am God of all people!"

"But Lord," I cried, "these Hutu are *not* people. They are demons, they are scorpions, they are worse than animals!"

His retort, within my heart, was sharp: "Who kept you alive for a hundred days?"

Faces passed before my mind: Marcel, Josephine, Louitpold, Toto, caring for us in the health center. Celestin, Thérèse, Annemarie, Saidi, Ezekias, risking their lives to save mine. They were all Hutu.

Understanding dawned: I am no different from anyone else – no, not different from the Hutu who killed our people. If I go against

God, I am just like those who killed and stole. Still kneeling, I cried, "Lord, what shall I do?"

Again the voice: "Denise, you survived only by grace. Give that grace to others! Forgive your pastor who betrayed his flock, the congregation who abandoned you, the killers who murdered your loved ones. If they harden their hearts and refuse to repent, that is my business. Your task is to help them become human again."

"Grace" was like a new word for me, one I still did not fully understand. But God was speaking, and I had to listen. My way of seeking guidance had always been to open the Bible at random and see what it told me. Western Christians have told me this approach is misguided, but the Bible was all I had. I opened it now and read from Acts 26:

> I have appeared to you to appoint you as a servant and as a witness of what you have seen and will see of me. I will rescue you from your own people and from the Gentiles. I am sending you to them to open their eyes and turn them from darkness to light, and from the power of Satan to God, so that they may receive forgiveness of sins and a place among those who are sanctified by faith in me.

I felt certain that these words, addressed to the apostle Paul, commissioned me too. Gentiles meant my Hutu neighbors. I believed Jesus wanted me to help them turn from darkness to light, from the power of Satan to God, so that they might receive forgiveness of their terrible sins against the Tutsi.

Throughout the genocide, I had accused God, doubting his love, succumbing to the thought that he loved only Hutu. Now, at last, I knew that he understood my inner battles and welcomed me as his child. His love overwhelmed me. Right then, I discovered I could genuinely pardon my Hutu neighbors. "Jesus does not want *anyone* to miss out on his mercy," I thought. I asked his forgiveness for my own anger and hatred. From this moment, fear no longer held me back; hate no longer pinned me down.

Still, it wouldn't always be easy. One day a young Hutu woman returning from a refugee camp in the Congo came to my door asking for clothes and food. My first thought was, "How can she dare to come to my home? Has she forgotten what they did to us?" But immediately the words of the Bible came to me: "Do not be overcome by evil, but overcome evil with good." I welcomed her in.

Eager now to seek reconciliation, I approached the official responsible for our area – or sector, as we call it – and asked him to summon the local population. Such gatherings are common in Rwandan villages. When he asked why I was requesting a meeting, I explained that neighbors had killed my friends and relatives – and pilfered my crops and possessions – earlier this year. They had not come to me, so I would take a step toward them. "If they confess their misdeeds, I will make peace," I said. "I am not looking for restitution, only for honesty."

He spread the word for everyone to gather in Nyakabuye, near the quarry where Charles had proposed to me. On the appointed day, the official brought a clipboard, paper, and pen. As everybody assembled for this outdoor meeting, each person involved wrote down what he or she had stolen from me.

When more than a hundred men and women had gathered, the official slowly read the list, name by name, with the description of what each had taken. When he finished, he asked me to speak. I looked around the assembly, from face to face, but everyone was looking at the rocky ground. No one would meet my eyes.

"Why didn't you come to see me, when you knew I had returned? Why did an official have to summon you to meet with me?" I began. "I knew exactly who killed my people and who took my things. I could have sued those of you who stole from my house. But I do not want revenge. I want to settle the matter personally and live in peace with you. How can we achieve this?"

There was silence. Then somebody called, "Forgive us!"

Other voices chimed in. "Forgive us! Please, forgive us!"

"Yes," I said, "I want to forgive you."

A woman threw up her hands, crying, "Oh! Denise forgives us, like Jesus on the cross!"

Reconciliation came at a price. Some survivors considered me a betrayer and accused me at the local military office. I was called in, and a soldier asked if it was true that I'd been communicating with Interahamwe.

Furious, I retorted, "Why didn't you wipe out all the Hutu when you liberated Bugarama? Then we wouldn't be having this conversation!"

"No," he said, "we are not going to kill them. We are a government of unity and reconciliation."

Calmer now, I replied, "Listen, I am a Christian. What future will this country have, if the killers don't have a chance to repent for what they've done? That's all I want." With a nod, my interrogator dismissed me.

THERE WOULD BE many more steps, through the years, on my forgiveness journey. The last week of the year 2000 brought a memorable one. I had no thought of anything unusual as I set off for a Kigali church on December 25; I simply hoped to show my gratitude to Theobald, who had stood by me in hard times. His son had just died in a motorcycle accident, and I was on my way to the funeral.

Thanks to traffic, I was late, and the priest was already speaking when I arrived. So, looking neither right nor left, I slipped quietly into a back-row seat. At the end of the service, as usual, the priest charged his congregation to pass on the greeting of peace. I turned to my left . . .

I was looking into the eyes of a former neighbor, a Cimerwa worker. His father had been a brazen killer, and his wife had looted my rooms. I had seen her parading through Bugarama with the leather purse Charles gave me as an engagement present. Some of my furniture was still in their house, I knew. Now I had to wish this man peace, and let go of any lingering resentment.

Is this your idea of a Christmas present, Jesus? Showing me I still held a grudge, making me wish peace to an enemy? Well, you scored this time!

I HAD TO LEAP another hurdle many years later, during a visit to the United States. I had been eager for this opportunity to meet relatives I hadn't seen since before the genocide. At Wheaton College, in Illinois, I was able to visit the Billy Graham Center, to honor the man whose witness in 1960 had been so decisive for my father, setting a positive direction for our whole family. I also went to New York City. I was impressed; but seeing its skyscrapers, I couldn't help thinking of widows I knew in Rwanda who had nowhere to shelter their children. "Couldn't America spare a scrap of its wealth to put roofs over my people?" I wondered.

My jolt came during a city tour, which I had not realized would include the UN headquarters. When we entered the building, I was slammed by the sight of United Nations soldiers. Fury flared within. I could taste it on my tongue.

In panic, I asked directions to the ladies' room, desperate to hide my turmoil. Locking myself in, I buried my head in my arms while bitter memories surged.

"Denise, have you heard? The UN has pulled out of Rwanda; no one cares what happens to you Tutsi!" – the sinister voice of Interahamwe lurking by the clinic sounded clear within my mind.

Yes, the UN had deserted my country at the critical hour, abandoning us to the slaughter. I had not realized this poisoned thorn still lodged in my heart, until the shock of seeing the familiar Blue Berets. When I had returned to Bugarama three months after the genocide, I had found United Nations peacekeepers camped on Cimerwa's soccer field. Their presence angered me so intensely, I had felt my hate as physical pain. "What are you doing here?" I had silently fumed. "Where were you when we needed you? You're too late – our people are dead!"

Charles and me on our wedding day, December 26, 1987

Visiting my parents in the Congo, August 1993. This is the only photo I have showing me (left), Charles (third from left), and our two young sons (front row).

Charles' mother and father (third and fifth from left) received a cow
as dowry at the wedding of their daughter Bellancille in August 1992.
Charles is at the far right.

My paternal grandparents, Ephraim and Damaris, with family. Of the
people in this photo only Uncle Eli (in black jacket) and his wife, Judith,
(in pink blouse) survived.

The house to the left is where we lived at the time of the genocide. This is the hole in the fence that I crawled through on April 16.

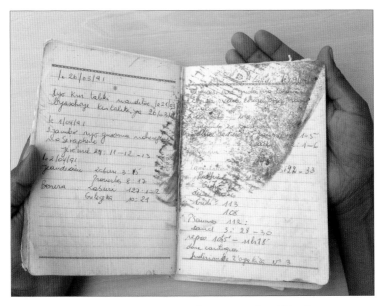

I found my journal with a footprint in dried blood.

Cimerwa Health Center, where we found refuge during the genocide

At the Gisozi memorial where Drocella's and Goretti's husbands are buried.
With me are Goretti, Ruth, Mapendo, Pascasie, and other Bugarama survivors.

Charles-Vital, Petit, and Christian with me, October 1994

I was presented with a lamp when I left Bugarama, January 1999

Survivors live with the effects of the genocide. Rukundo, whose arm was cut off when she was a baby, lost her parents and all her relatives.

Sisterhood: Beata, me, and Drocella, 2018

Lautharie

Jeanne, a Solace coworker, lost her husband and five children in the genocide.

Antoine Rutayisire

A cow given to a former-Tutsi widow had a calf. Now Drocella is giving the
calf to a former-Hutu woman.

Dancing for joy

Peacemaker women of Shalom Ministries – women work side by side to
prepare earth for planting.

Theresie (right), and another Mukoma mother show me the site where seventy-three baby boys were massacred.

Visiting Gaudence, who lost eight of nine children, and her granddaughter in Mukoma, 2018

Comforting a Mukoma widow on a home visit

Outside the makeshift tent the Mukoma widows built for their gatherings,
August 2011

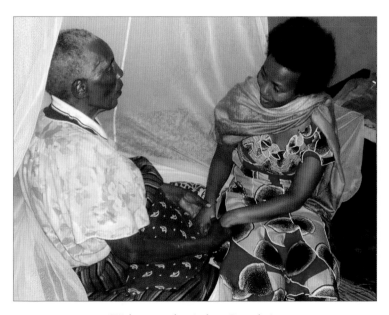

With my mother-in-law, Consoletia

Learning love instead of hate – children at the Iriba Shalom center in Mukoma

At the opening ceremony for the Iriba Shalom center, in background, Consoletia and four other widows received a cow, August 2018.

Cancilde, left, and others who have forgiven their families' killers, April 2015

With Cancilde, Emmanuel, and Wolfgang, August 2015

Mukoma widows and orphans build a house for a widow.

Children of reconciliation, Mukoma.

The diplomats here at UN headquarters were even more to blame than the troops on the ground. In January 1994, when General Roméo Dallaire learned that Interahamwe were amassing weapons, he wanted to confiscate them, to prevent mass murder. But his superiors, right here in New York City, forbade him. Dallaire said that if he had had 5,500 troops, he could have prevented the genocide. Yet on April 21, 1994, the United Nations cut its forces in Rwanda by ninety percent, to only 270 soldiers. Finally, in mid-May, UN leaders resolved to send more troops – but then delayed while quibbling over who would pay. They had even refused to use the term "genocide" for weeks, while over a million Tutsi were killed, because acknowledging the fact would have obliged them to intervene.

Their indifference had cost my husband his life, as well as all the others. How could I cope with my rage? Shaking, I pulled the tiny Bible from my purse. It opened to Isaiah 49. "Can a mother forget the baby at her breast and have no compassion on the child she has borne?" I read. "Though she may forget, I will not forget you!"

The United Nations was meant to care for all the countries of the earth, yet it forgot us in our need. But you, Lord, did not. Is that what you are telling me?

Calmer now, I left the bathroom. Following an inner urge, I requested the UN visitors' book and picked up the pen. Resolutely, I wrote, "I was angry against the United Nations, because you left us alone during the genocide against the Tutsi in Rwanda. Today I forgive you. But I ask you to support widows and orphans, especially women who were raped and have HIV." Then I wrote the date – October 21, 2009 – and signed my name.

They say forgiving is an ongoing process, a daily battle, and that's certainly how the last twenty-five years have been for me. But, as I would soon discover, it wasn't a journey I would have to make alone – thousands were on the road with me.

13

Mukoma

AFTER RECONCILING with my Bugarama neighbors, I often found my thoughts turning to my mother-in-law, who had lost her husband, a daughter, and seven of her eight sons in the genocide. Consoletia had moved back home since I had found her, broken, in Kigali. I felt an obligation toward my husband's mother and wanted to see how she was doing.

I recoiled at the thought of taking my children to her village, however. The region along Lake Kivu's shore was still raided by Hutu militias from the Congo. Mukoma had no electricity, and I shuddered to imagine dark nights with marauders prowling outside.

Then, early in 1996, an inner voice overcame my misgivings: "Denise, I am not only God where there is electricity!"

Ashamed of my fears, I took Charles-Vital, Christian, and Petit to spend a long weekend with Consoletia. I did not know how to encourage this mother and grandmother who had lost so much, but at least we could show her our love and respect.

After an hour and a half on the bus, we arrived in Mukoma. The blue sky still arched overhead; the blue lake still glistened below. Other than that, I would not have recognized the place I had delighted to visit with Charles during our courtship. Fields were bare of crops or overgrown with weeds, banana groves were unkempt, and charred smudges were all that remained where picturesque huts had dotted the hillsides.

Gone were the lowing cattle and laughing voices. The few children we met looked at us from sullen, mistrustful eyes.

We made our way through the devastation to Consoletia's compound. It was nothing like the grand place of the past, but at least she had a home. She welcomed us warmly and served the meager meal she had prepared.

Then my boys went out to play. My mother-in-law and I sat outside her door, watching them. At first we hardly spoke. Then her friend Theresie joined us, and, haltingly, the two of them described what had happened here.

"Callixte and I invested all our time, resources, and energy in our eleven children," Consoletia said. "They were our hope for the future. For some years after the 1973 crisis, everything seemed peaceful. We got along well with the few Hutu in Mukoma. We gave them cows, cementing our bond of friendship. Callixte and I were godparents for several Hutu children."

She paused over her memories, then continued, "In 1990, when the war of liberation began, we Tutsi were accused of supporting the RPF. Hutu neighbors claimed my husband and I had sent our sons out of the country to join the rebels, though in reality we had sent them to study."

"Then came 1994," Theresie interjected. "On April 7, just after my husband and I heard that President Habyarimana's plane had been shot down, Hutu neighbors started seizing our cows and goats. Two days later, our house was set on fire. We picked up our two small sons and hurried here, to our friends Consoletia and Callixte.

Then Interahamwe started invading from other districts. At first, most of Mukoma's Hutu joined us Tutsi, to fight off these raids."

Theresie and her family were not the only ones to rush to my relatives' large compound. Tutsi homes were torched throughout the region, and many of their inhabitants fled to Callixte and Consoletia's place. Although Mukoma villagers – Tutsi and Hutu together – at first fended off the attack, on April 11 Interahamwe started throwing grenades, and several people were killed.

First thing in the morning on April 12, Mukoma's mayor summoned all the men to a "peace meeting" in the large village hall. Two farmers missed this meeting; by mid-morning, they would be the only Tutsi men alive. After the men of the village had assembled, all Hutu were ordered out of the hall. Then the room was locked, gasoline was poured onto the building, and it was set ablaze. The few who escaped the flames were slain with machetes. Three hundred men died that morning.

Around ten o'clock, the women at my mother-in-law's place realized what had just happened. But before they could grasp it or devise a plan, Interahamwe came after them and their children.

Theresie now told me, "Hutu militia attacked Consoletia's compound, singing '*Tuza batsembe tsembe.*' We locked ourselves in, but they broke down the door. With clubs and machetes, they killed nineteen mothers and twenty-five children. The women who were not killed were raped."

Theresie could hardly speak, but she clearly wanted the truth to be known. "The next day," she said, "other mothers and I were forced to bring our baby boys and watch them being killed. Both my little sons were murdered that day, with seventy-one others. Altogether, 546 people were killed in Mukoma."

My mother-in-law did not see the dreadful massacre of infants, but she witnessed many of the forty-four deaths in her home. One was a little grandchild. Another was her daughter, Mary – yes, my dear Mary, who stood by me when Christian was born. While killing her, Interahamwe had quipped that they were preventing this young lady from becoming a cook for the RPF.

Consoletia's seventeen-year-old son – home from the Congo for Easter vacation – was also killed, betrayed by a classmate.

Consoletia herself was beaten outside her house "from head to foot," stripped of her clothes, and left for dead. A passing neighbor covered her, but she lay in the rain for three days and nights, hearing the cries of children begging for help, and for water, until they died. Consoletia went into a coma.

A Hutu neighbor finally took my mother-in-law home. She eventually regained consciousness and was taken to Nyarushishi Refugee Camp. From there – after liberation – UNHCR brought her to Kigali, where she and I had met. As I had seen, she had been miserable there; so when she was able, she returned to Mukoma. Her one living son, Jean, who had been an RPF soldier, helped her rebuild the house and plant some crops.

Darkness had settled over land and lake by the time Consoletia and Theresie finished talking, yet we three sat for a long time – they brooding on their memories, I silenced by their suffering.

During the days I spent in Mukoma, I met indifference and suspicion wherever I walked – even though I had been known here since before my wedding to Charles, who had grown up in this place. I realized this community was still living in the genocide. The men and boys had been killed. The women and girls had been so debased, they looked out on life through dead or angry eyes.

Almost everyone here, it seemed, had lost their faith, their lives a meaningless grind from day to day. A young widow, Lautharie, was typical. Having been slashed and thrown into a latrine to die after her husband and children were killed, she now hated the Shangi parish priest, who had joined the killing after intoning pious prayers, and his Hutu congregants, who had sung holy hymns and then refused to hide their neighbors.

Lautharie returned to church just once, to shout, "Don't you touch that bread and wine with blood on your hands!"

An alarming number of Mukoma's women were ill. Only years later was their condition diagnosed as AIDS, contracted while being raped.

Rather than turning to each other for comfort, most women isolated themselves. Many tried to dull their pain with banana beer they brewed. At least one went insane.

After our three-day visit, I took my boys home to Bugarama, deeply troubled by all I had seen and heard in Mukoma.

TIME PASSED. On Monday evenings, Louitpold, Josephine, and Felix always came to encourage, support, and pray with me. I participated in the life of Bugarama – volunteering in the choir, supporting returning Hutu refugees, getting up early to carry rocks from the river to help build a church, visiting widows and orphans – but life remained a daily challenge.

I continued to meet weekly with five other surviving Tutsi women in Bugarama. We shared our needs and supported the most vulnerable among us. Each of us took in orphans. And every year we organized a special commemoration on April 16, to observe the day genocide had swept our town.

On January 9, 1997, Paul Kagame visited Bugarama to tour the factory. He would become Rwanda's president in 2000, but was vice president at the time. Cement production is a vital industry in Rwanda, where there are few exportable resources, and Cimerwa belongs to the government. It was an honor for the company to host this leader and an honor for me to be assigned to serve him and the men who came with him. As I poured Mr. Kagame a glass of Sprite, we exchanged a few words. Since others were present, I could not freely speak my mind; I would have liked to express my sincere thanks to this freedom fighter, because many more Tutsi – including my children and me – would likely have died had he not led the RPF to victory over the genocide government.

One day in 1998, Cimerwa's Bugarama management threatened to evict another Tutsi woman and me from our company-owned homes, because we did not have a spouse also working for Cimerwa. It was painful to realize there was still animosity toward us. That night, and many subsequent nights, I went to an empty goat shed behind my house to pray.

"It's too much," I prayed. "Please let me leave! Pick me up, and throw me far away from here – to some place where I can breathe freely."

One morning, after such a night of prayer, I lifted the rug from the shed's floor – and a viper slithered from beneath it. I had been kneeling for hours on a deadly snake. I took this as a reminder that God was in control.

ON JANUARY 11, 1999, Cimerwa's Chinese director called me in. He asked if I would be willing to relocate to a new depot the company was opening in Kigali.

I accepted immediately, believing the time had come to move on. I did not want to leave Bugarama, however, without making peace with everyone. I was to depart in three weeks.

When my coworkers learned that I was going, many came offering help. Some harvested my rice, corn, and sorghum, and a Cimerwa truck driver transported these crops from my allotment. One of the ladies washed my laundry and ironed clothes, while others cleaned the house and helped me pack.

Friends came to pray for my move, and I invited others, to say goodbye. I was particularly touched when one of them presented a lovely lamp as a farewell gift, saying, "Denise, you were a light for us!"

Looking back over my life in Bugarama, I felt physically and emotionally drained, in dire need of renewal. I was more than ready to leave, after all my heartbreak and struggle in this place.

Yet I was thankful God had sent me here eleven years ago, so I could meet and marry Charles and build a family with him. And I was thankful God had sent me back after the genocide, to reconcile with everyone here. Bugarama had refined me, like travertine in Cimerwa's kiln.

14

The Sisterhood

MY SONS AND I MOVED to the capital in February 1999.
Evelyn, one of the Bugarama orphans I had taken in, came with us.
Like Charles-Vital, she was nine years old. Christian was six, and
Petit was almost five.

Although Cimerwa offered accommodation, I decided instead
to rejoin my parents and extended family, who were still in Kigali.
My brother, Clement, helped find a private school for the children.
I was determined to do my utmost for them, as I had promised
Charles.

I soon took up work responsibilities at the new warehouse, where
I had been made general manager. By this time, the government
had abolished the terms "Hutu" and "Tutsi" – we were all simply
Rwandan. But the ten workers I supervised were former Hutu,
and at first they looked at me askance, wondering what to expect
from a genocide survivor. I soon won their trust, however. Cement
sales were booming in this time of rebuilding, with new customers
arriving at the door each day. I treated everyone with equal respect,

from the president's representative to the poorest people trying to rebuild their burned-down homes.

On a practical level, things were going well. I received a good salary, had a car and driver at my disposal, and was sending my boys to an excellent school. My spirit, however, was far from healed. I pined for my missing husband. Five years had passed since the genocide, but I still vomited every day and had repeated nightmares of Interahamwe chasing me down or killing my children. Often I wondered what would give life meaning here. I felt an almost physical thirst for God. During my lunch break, I would slip away to a prayer meeting at a nearby Baptist church.

At seven o'clock each morning, I led a brief devotion for our warehouse team. Three of the workers were eventually baptized, having given their lives to Christ through these gatherings. A few customers started coming early to take part as well. One morning, however, an official arrived from the Ministry of Mining and Industry, to which Cimerwa was accountable. Finding a prayer meeting underway, he reproached me.

"Who gave you permission to pray in a public office?" he demanded.

"I have to pray before starting work," I replied.

"That's against the rules," he snapped.

Marching into my supervisor's office, he said, "Your colleague is praying instead of working."

"No, Denise does her job well," my Chinese boss countered calmly. "She gathers her employees before hours. Then they get to work punctually."

My coworkers were gleeful. "Oh Denise, your God vindicated you," one of them exulted.

The next day the official showed up to buy cement from me, and he became a regular customer. Every time he came through the door, I was reminded that government officials also need our prayers.

Half a year later, a new customer entered. Noticing the Bible on my desk, he commented, "That's a great book." I agreed but continued my work, maintaining the reserve I had established in this male-dominated business world.

It wasn't long before the man returned for more cement. Again he picked up my Bible, repeating, "Nice book!"

To prevent conversation, I said, "Do you know who I am? I'm a survivor of the genocide against the Tutsi, and I'm a Christian."

That would have been enough to silence most people. Instead Jean Gakwandi – as the customer introduced himself – said that he and his wife, Viviane, were also former Tutsi who had miraculously lived through 1994. They believed God had spared their lives so they could support other survivors, and they had started building a center where widows and orphans could receive care and find comfort. That was why he kept coming for building materials. They called their endeavor Solace Ministries.

My heart kindled as Jean spoke of homes to rebuild, traumatized souls to comfort, AIDS victims to care for, orphaned children to feed and educate. Might this be an answer to my quest for purpose? I was so stirred by his words, I donated five sacks of cement, paid from my salary.

Jean invited me to a meeting of survivors. I accepted, and the following Saturday he drove the children and me forty-five minutes east to Rwamagana. A young widowed social worker, Rose, came along. She worked with AVEGA, an umbrella organization that helped genocide widows and their families return to normalcy and receive the aid they were entitled to.

Odetta, who represented AVEGA in Rwanda's eastern region, had organized this survivors' meeting, spreading the word far and wide, and she welcomed us when our car pulled up. Greeting me warmly, she asked about my 1994 experience. As I told her what I had been through, it was a relief to weep with another woman who had lost her husband. We could not converse long, however, because others were arriving, and Odetta wanted to welcome them too.

For nearly an hour, I sat on the open hillside, quietly watching as perhaps five hundred women arrived, on foot, from every direction. Some had set out before daybreak to be at this gathering. Their faces revealed the emptiness each was suffering; they had all lost people whose lives gave meaning to their own.

When the meeting began, Odetta asked me to speak. I told these women that I did not know what had become of my husband, and that my youngest child had been born while the Tutsi in my town were being slain. Tears streamed down my listeners' faces as their own memories resurfaced. But our pain brought us close, and I ended by declaring my certainty that God had saved each of us for a purpose.

Some of the women came up afterward to talk. "Where do you, such a young woman, find strength to hearten the rest of us?" one asked.

"Jesus helps me," I replied, "though I'm still bruised, like you."

On Sundays, in Kigali, I joined meetings of forty or fifty widows. Eventually we were able to use the center for which I had helped provide cement. Beata Mukarubuga, a Solace volunteer, always had someone contribute an encouraging message at these gatherings, and anyone could bring others along. There was a warmth among us, and a depth of inner peace, that I had not known in a long time. "It's like a cooking fire," I thought. "When smoldering sticks are scattered, they smoke and go out – but if they're brought together, they flare into flame."

During the week, Solace invited survivors to attend a regular Wednesday meeting. Whenever it was my turn to set these up, Charles-Vital, Evelyn, Christian, and Petit swept the room and decorated it with flowers so everyone would feel honored and welcome. Then they placed chairs in a circle.

While we mothers met, our children would play nearby. Although we worried about their future, their shouts and laughter encouraged us. If they could rise above the past, perhaps someday we would too.

When widows started seeking me out at my workplace, I began to realize the extent of the need. My boss gave me time off to visit these women and their children. There were many child-led households: an older child caring for younger ones when both parents were dead. Solace provided me with a way to help them, and, as my financial situation improved, I donated all I could to this ministry.

For the previous five years, I had thought my problems severe. Now, I realized how fortunate I was. Yes, my husband was gone, and nothing could erase that pain or fill the gap he had left in my life. But my children were alive; countless mothers had lost all their loved ones. My children and I were healthy and whole, unlike the survivors I saw with scarred faces and disfigured bodies.

And I had not been raped. I was a rare exception, because rape had been a deliberate Interahamwe tactic. Almost all surviving Tutsi women and girls had endured it. Many were infected with HIV. Amnesty International's report, "Marked for Death: Rape Survivors Living with HIV/AIDS in Rwanda," states, "According to a UN report, at least 250,000 women were raped. . . . Of the survivors, 70 percent are estimated to have been infected with HIV."

The remnant of our people were dealing with seething rage, on top of grief and hopelessness. Some survivors now called all former Hutu *inyamaswa*, "animals." For too many, the future seemed meaningless. "Why should I go to school?" I heard a child ask. "My father was an engineer. He's dead. My brothers and sisters all went to school. They're dead too."

Thousands agonized over not knowing what had become of loved ones. Unable to learn their fate – or honor them in burial and grieve at their graves – we could not free ourselves from tormenting images of their bodies thrown into some horrible pit or torn to pieces by dogs or by the carrion-eating kites we still saw hovering over our land.

Some victims resented the food and blankets provided by international agencies. "Where were you Americans and Europeans when we needed you?" they asked.

But others rejected aid out of a sense of guilt. "How can I cook and eat alone?" one widow, Mukamazi, questioned. "Have I become so selfish that I can eat, when my husband and children are dead? I don't deserve to live!" In the end, she took her own life.

FRANCINE UMURUNGI was one of hundreds who appeared at Solace Ministries' door. The first time she came, her eyes were dull.

"I felt I was walking dead," she told me, much later. "I hated God, all Hutu, and the child I bore. I was deeply depressed and very, very desperate." She had made at least one suicide attempt.

Before rape and genocide destroyed her world at age thirteen, Francine had never imagined life could be ugly. One of eight children in a lively home, she had been a vivacious, carefree girl. Francine's family lived comfortably from their crops and from their cows, goats, and poultry. Her father was a teacher, and her mother ran the farm with the older children.

After the genocide, Francine and her few remaining siblings crowded in with an aunt in Kigali. Here Francine spiraled downward. Repulsed by life, herself, and other people, she rejected all hope. Her aunt begged her to visit Solace, but "I only wanted death, and I kept refusing to go," she recalled.

Francine later said, "I wanted to ask God: 'Where were you when the soldier raped me? Where were you when my parents were murdered? Where were you when I stood in line with all those naked women, waiting to be thrown into that ghastly grave seething with dead and half-dead bodies?'"

Living in fear of every man, Francine tried to make herself invisible. Debilitated by AIDS, she steadily lost weight and developed skin disease. Meanwhile, the emotional acid in her heart was corroding her life from within, year after year.

Finally Francine came to Solace, to silence her aunt's nagging. She arrived at ten o'clock that morning, declaring, "Before we speak, let me tell you three things. Don't ask me to love God, because he deserted me. Don't ask me to love the Hutu, because they made me what I am. And don't tell me to love the child I bore through rape. I hate her!"

Then Francine began to talk. Every vile memory she had repressed poured out, an unabated toxic torrent.

When her words and weeping ceased three hours later, the tension and defiance she had brought into the building were gone. She later said that after years of torment, telling everything had brought indescribable relief. We prayed with her.

Francine came regularly from then on, to attend our gatherings and to receive ongoing care and counseling. Solace funded anti-retroviral treatment and refurbished a simple house for her to share with her daughter and siblings.

"They made me feel that I was worth something – that I wasn't just a piece of garbage," she says.

A few years later, I received a phone call from Jean Gakwandi. "Pray that Francine Umurungi doesn't die," he said. "She is in the hospital, extremely ill."

It was difficult to get regular medication for AIDS back then, and Francine was wasting away. But all the Solace widows prayed for her, and she eventually recovered enough to go home. I visited her there, and she cooked me a simple meal – a sign that she was healing emotionally as well as physically.

In 2018 we managed to reconnect. She told me that learning to love her daughter – herself now a young woman – has taken all these years. Francine's siblings had always detested the girl, because the rapist who fathered her was the brother of the man who killed their mother.

"It's been so hard for us to really get to know each other," Francine told me. "We've both been so deeply hurt. But we're both determined."

Francine said her daughter had pleaded to know the date of her birth; all her life, she had watched other girls celebrate their birthdays, and she didn't even know hers.

Francine felt she had failed utterly, and she wept when her daughter said, "Mama, I understand your difficult situation."

"You hold the key to your daughter's heart," I assured her. "Someday it will open fully to you. Don't give up!"

In February 2000, I attended a five-day counseling seminar. So far, my support for other survivors had consisted of listening – and of weeping and praying together. I had often wished I had more knowledge, and I hoped this brief course might give me some ideas.

The young woman sitting beside me worked for AVEGA, and we got along well. Her name was Drocella Nduwimana.

At one point during the workshop, we suddenly found ourselves laughing. The American instructor had just recommended that each attendee create a five-year plan. Drocella and I looked at each other in disbelief. We were glad to make it through one day, let alone five years!

The others must have felt the same, because the suggestion met blank silence, until a young widow blurted, "I created a five-year plan, with my husband. It didn't work!"

That's when the hilarity erupted. I felt sorry for the foreigner, who seemed shocked by our response. But laughing sure felt good – the first time in six years.

My friendship with Drocella deepened when she told me her story. She had grown up in Gisagara, in the south-central part of the country. Her father sent her to Burundi after elementary school, because of the Rwandan laws barring Tutsi from higher education. Drocella eventually graduated from college there, and she stayed in Burundi to teach, since her degree was not recognized back home.

In 1988, however, she decided to return to Rwanda. She switched her career to accounting and took a job with a utilities firm in Kigali.

In 1993, she married Daniel Ntagwabira there. Shyly, Drocella took out a photo of the two of them surrounded by friends on their wedding day – she in white, he in a tuxedo. The honeymoon glow had not faded when the genocide hit, half a year later.

The very first day, on April 7, a Hutu neighbor agreed to hide Drocella – but not Daniel. He was killed at home three days later. Drocella was informed of his death, but she could not go next door to prepare his body for burial or even to see her young husband's face once more. She was beside herself.

The neighbor brought Daniel's wedding ring, messy with blood. But the disgust with which she presented it made Drocella feel she had no right to show any emotion. So she clamped her feelings inside. She dared not dwell on the moment, seven months before, when she had placed that ring on Daniel's finger.

Two days later, her hostess ordered her to leave, afraid of being discovered harboring a Tutsi. She did one last kindness, though, getting Drocella a place in a vehicle evacuating military wives from Kigali.

Arriving in her old home, Drocella thought she had cheated death. Life appeared almost normal in Gisagara. No corner of our country was spared, however, and the violence soon spread south. On April 21, Drocella fled with her mother and some of her sisters to nearby Burundi.

On returning to Gisagara three months later, when the bloodshed was over, Drocella learned that all of her family who had stayed in Rwanda had perished: an older sister with her husband and five children, a brother with his wife and son, and other relatives. All their homes had been destroyed, their cattle killed, their belongings taken. There was nothing for remaining family members to start over with.

With no time to grieve her loved ones, Drocella returned to the chaos of post-genocide Kigali. It was extremely difficult to be back in this familiar yet irrevocably changed city, and it was especially unnerving to meet relatives of Daniel's killers. She knew who they were, and they would turn up on the street when she least expected them.

Back at work, she avoided a Hutu coworker, suspecting her of murder. But Drocella got together with other colleagues, widowed survivors like herself, to compare experiences, to lament, and to condemn the killers.

None of these young women was coping with her loss. In an effort to numb their pain, some started taking sleeping pills or experimenting with street drugs and alcohol. Drocella, too, lacked spirit to restart life alone. "Why am I even alive?" she asked God.

Four months after returning to Kigali, while searching her Bible for answers, Drocella came across a verse, in Paul's First Letter to Timothy, that spoke to her: "She who is truly a widow, left all alone, has set her hope on God and continues in supplications and prayers night and day, but she who is self-indulgent is dead even while she lives."

Drocella felt certain that Daniel would not want her succumbing to self-pity and pessimism. So she fasted, praying for peace and asking to be shown how to help the others.

At her workplace, she told two other young widows what she had discovered in scripture, and they began meeting for prayer during lunch break. "We shared the word of God," Drocella explained. "Through that word, God healed our wounds step by step, and brought peace to our broken hearts."

In the office, Hutu colleagues began noticing the change. "What happened to you?" one inquired. "Can we join your meeting?" another asked.

Realizing that everyone needs peace, no matter which side of the conflict they had been on, Drocella welcomed them. She named the group Shalom Ministries; it continues to this day.

"After experiencing this healing," Drocella added, "I forgave the people who killed my husband and family."

That was too much for me. It's one thing to forgive people who pilfer your possessions, but something else entirely to forgive those who murder your loved ones.

"*How* did you forgive your husband's killers?" I broke in.

American journalist Stephen Kinzer ran into the same question. In his book *A Thousand Hills*, he asks, "How have so many Rwandans come to forgive those who trespassed so terribly against them? Most of those I met gave me the same answer: this is what God wants." Kinzer concludes, "The depth of forgiveness being asked of Rwandans can be understood only in a spiritual context, not a rational one."

That's what I discovered when I questioned Drocella. "God did a miracle," she answered simply. "That's why I continue to praise him. Hallelujah!"

She and I kept up our friendship after the seminar ended, and it wasn't long before I turned to her for help. Space was tight in my parents' house, where I had moved in with Evelyn and my three sons. So when several more orphans came to the door, pleading to join me, I called Drocella.

"Send them to me!" she responded.

Now, more than two decades on, she says, "When my husband was killed, I was thirty-one years old – a widow without a child. Yet I have never been alone in my home. I have had many sons and daughters to care for and love. They've all grown up now. Some have graduated from college, and some have married. One of these days, I'll be a grandmother!"

Drocella eventually decided to give all her time to Shalom Ministries, with its goal of healing families and communities. In the south of the country, her home area, she started gathering women of four situations: Tutsi women whose Tutsi husbands had been killed, Hutu women whose Tutsi husbands had been killed, Hutu women whose Hutu husbands are in prison, and Tutsi women whose Hutu husbands are in prison.

At first, their animosity was such that the genocide widows would go to prisons with the sole intent of preventing "prison widows" from bringing food to their husbands. I, too, had witnessed the intensity of hate between these factions, so I asked, "How did you reconcile them?"

"I had started approaching Tutsi women about forgiveness, back when I worked for AVEGA," Drocella replied. "It was easy for them to listen to me, because I was one of their number. Then I spoke similarly to the other groups. It took time. But when they eventually met, they discovered how much they had in common."

Drocella added, "We gather together, we work together, and we pray together. Since Jesus is the center of our work, we call ourselves Peacemaker Women."

She and I share the work to this day, even across vast distances. My organization in Europe helps provide cattle, which Drocella and other Peacemaker Women of Shalom Ministries bring to the villages. They give a cow to a widow of Tutsi background, who gives its calf to a widow of Hutu origin, and so on.

"I'm a queen," one widow exclaimed to Drocella. "King Jesus has given me a cow!"

15

Beata

IN AUGUST 2000, Solace Ministries' leaders sent four of us
volunteers to a conference in Kenya, hoping it would stimulate and
inspire us. The event, put on by the Anglican Church in Kenya,
was attended by Christians from many countries and denomina-
tions. It was good to see the acceptance and unity among people of
differing ethnic groups.

The greatest benefit of the trip, however, was having time to
get more deeply acquainted with my own companions. We traveled more than seven hundred miles each way, so Drocella, Beata,
Anasthasie, and I had plenty of time to talk on the bus.

From my first encounter with Beata Mukarubuga the year
before, I had felt a special respect for her – and not only because
she was twelve years my elder. She attracted hurting souls like a
hen drawing frightened chicks under its wings. I took the opportunity of this long journey to ask for her story.

Born in 1952, Beata spent her girlhood in Nyanza, southern
Rwanda, where her father owned a large dairy herd. Since she

enjoyed looking after her younger brothers and sisters, she became a teacher. In 1978, she married Placide, a school principal, and they eventually had eight children. As matters turned out, having been a teacher saved Beata's life.

Like me, Beata learned of President Habyarimana's assassination when hailing a neighbor on the morning of April 7. Our Kinyarwanda greeting *Muracyariho?* means "Are you still alive?" This time, however, her neighbor said, "Why are you still alive?" Then, accusingly – as if she had launched it – he told her that the previous evening a missile had demolished the president's jet, killing him and his companions.

Beata hurried home. "We had better leave Rwanda," she said, after telling her husband the news.

"Let's hang on and see what happens," Placide responded. "We're not the only Tutsi around here." He had never been one for hasty action.

For nearly two weeks, staying home seemed to have been the right decision. Most Hutu in Nyanza refused to join the madness. While atrocities were multiplying across Rwanda, Beata's area remained relatively calm, if tense.

Other Tutsi began arriving from surrounding provinces seeking refuge, some herding their cattle before them. Hundreds of these people camped on Mount Gacu, not far from Beata's home.

The nation's extremist Hutu leaders were incensed that one province defied their plan for total annihilation of the Tutsi. On April 18, determined to reverse the situation, they summoned Nyanza's local government leaders to a meeting. President Sindikubwabo, who had replaced Habyarimana, came down from Kigali himself for the consultation.

Beata never heard what transpired behind the meeting's closed doors, but matters quickly worsened in Nyanza. On April 21, her uneasiness grew when she noticed smoke rising over nearby hills. That same day, checkpoints were established at intervals along all the byways throughout the area, as they had been on nearly every road in Rwanda.

"Checkpoint" is a euphemism. These were killing stations. Guards demanded to know the identity of every passerby. Anyone with a Tutsi ID card – or no card – was meant to be killed on the spot, with no further questions asked. All Hutu men and boys were required to do their stint at these barriers. Organizers went from one Hutu home to the next, detailing guard shifts. Roadblock sentries were supplied with beer, and most kept a radio going. From a distance, Beata could hear them singing along with RTLM's popular hate songs.

On April 22, the military police descended. *Tuza batsembe tsembe*, "We will exterminate them!" they chanted on Mount Gacu while slaughtering the Tutsi's cattle – a profane act in our culture.

When the cows were dead, the killers turned on the people. Beata heard gunfire through that night as refugees were chased down. Some escaped from the ridge to swamps and forests, but national attention was now focused on the region. "Cut down Nyanza's tall trees!" screeched RTLM. Everyone knew "tall trees" was code for Tutsi men.

Next morning, Beata's husband hurried to a local official who had helped him during the unrest in 1990. Placide had been jailed back then, just like Charles. But this time the official said the only help he could offer was for Placide and his family to be killed with bullets rather than machetes, because national policy decreed that every Tutsi must die.

Rushing home with this grim report, Placide found a Hutu neighbor at the door, begging Beata to flee. "People are being killed everywhere, and your names are on the list," the woman was crying. "They plan to use gasoline from your husband's motorbike to burn down your house!"

Again Placide hesitated. It was the worst, and last, mistake of his life. In minutes, a truck pulled up, driven by a local businessman,

Japhet. There were several Tutsi men in the back of the truck, and Japhet instructed Placide to join them. He obeyed. The truck drove off. Beata never saw her husband again.

BEATA HAD TO ACT FAST. She immediately sent three of her children with the woman who had just raised the alarm, one with the housegirl, one to his Hutu godfather, and two others to hide with an elderly Tutsi man she believed would be respected.

Then she tied her youngest child, one-year-old Lambert, onto her back and fled herself. But wherever she went, people turned her away, saying her child would bring danger by crying. So she hid in the woods, trying to shield her small son from the heavy April rains with his *ingobyi*.

On the morning of April 28, she heard Interahamwe searching the brush. Fortunately she knew the area better than they did and gave them the slip. But they caught a young acquaintance, and she heard him crying, "I'm innocent, I'm innocent," while they beat him to death.

Now she fled to the hut of a God-fearing Hutu, Isaka, who hid her for several days. But one night he heard that killers had learned of her whereabouts and planned to come for her in the morning; they were efficient, keeping account of every Tutsi in Nyanza. Waking Beata at three o'clock, Isaka told her to disappear into the dark. Before she left, he gave her some food and a Bible.

"Do you think those who died didn't have Bibles?" Beata asked, incredulous. "Rather give me a gun or grenade!"

The following weeks consisted of hiding – in swamps, forests, sorghum fields, and tea plantations. Interahamwe patrolled the whole province, hunting woods and croplands, using dogs and whistles to track down survivors. A dog found Beata and her son, but she hit it hard on the head with her Bible, and it bolted.

Beata ran and fell, ran and fell. Sharp grasses cut her hands and stones bruised her body. When trying to swim across a river with

Beata

Lambert on her back, she was caught by the current and swept downstream. They nearly drowned. Often, in the coming months and years, she wished they had.

Sometimes Beata was able to glean crops from the fields where they hid, but on occasion she had to creep from cover for food. One of these times, some of her neighbors spotted her and raised a cry. Hearing their shouts, she fled into a local pottery. The Twa woman who ran the place hid Beata and Lambert behind a row of big earthenware pots.

When her pursuers arrived, asking if a Tutsi woman had entered, Beata recognized several of their voices. Her heart was pounding so loudly, she thought she was hearing their footsteps approaching her hiding place. But the potter responded with scorn.

"You Hutu – you must be kidding!" she scoffed. "*You're* the ones who used to eat and drink with Tutsi. We Twa never had anything to do with those snakes."

"I wish your Tutsi lady *were* here," she added. "Then at least I could have her clothes when you killed her." Convinced by the woman's bluff, the pack moved off to search elsewhere.

The ceramic worker called the fugitives out of hiding to share a meal of sorghum porridge. Beata hoped that at last she had found safe haven.

But it was not to be. The woman's son soon appeared, laden with clothing and goods from the homes of murdered Tutsi. Livid at finding surviving Tutsi in his own home, he took his traditional sword and would have killed Beata and Lambert right then. But the lady again intervened, pleading for their lives.

"Oh, all right," her son relented. "But get them out of this house."

At last Beata's luck seemed to have failed. A company of Interahamwe caught her and Lambert almost immediately. They had captured about eighty Tutsi and now led them to a deep trench and made them stand along its edge – men and boys in one line, women and girls in another. Then, at their leader's signal, they took up

151

their machetes and began to swing and strike, slashing their way down the row, pushing the dead and dying into the grave.

This is Beata's worst memory: the horrible sounds of death strokes on human skulls and bodies, screams of agony and terror, pleading cries of children, harsh rejoinders of killers, prayers cut off mid-syllable. A child's shriek, "I'll tell my papa if you kill me!" was followed by a fiendish guffaw and hideous thud.

Frozen, Beata waited her turn. When only four people remained between her and death, a killer grabbed her arm and jerked her from the line, yelling, "How did you get here, Beata Mukarubuga? I'll kill you my own way!" As the teenager pulled her into the bushes, she recognized him – a former student.

"I don't want to see you sliced up," he hissed. "Get away! Stay in the bushes. All houses will be searched. But you'll die anyhow. No Tutsi will survive." He gave her a shove.

SO THE TERRIFYING GAME continued. Beata tried to care for her little boy in the hills around Gatagara. Lambert would cry, "Milk, Mama, milk!" or "I want Papa!" Occasionally he called, "Olivier, Claudette, where are you?" – his favorite brother and sister. But as Beata continued to slip from one hiding place to the next, he became floppy, dozing most of the time. The mother's desperation grew. It was mid-May by now, and she had been on the run for nearly a month.

"Lord, if we Tutsi have sinned, please forgive us," Beata cried. "But see how my little one is starving!" She herself was weak from hunger and thirst and had difficulty thinking clearly. She was still carrying the Bible on her back with her child. "Why am I toting this useless, heavy book?" she thought.

With a flash of anger, she flung it as far as she could. Following it with her eyes, she saw that the tangled thicket where it fell was heavy with *inkeri*, the edible berries her family used to harvest from the woods. Wading through, she salvaged the Bible and started picking, squeezing *inkeri* into Lambert's mouth and eating handfuls herself. He revived in hours. The berries were so plentiful, she and her son lived on them for eleven days.

But they could not survive in the bush forever. Finally Beata ventured out, to the home of someone to whom her husband had once given a cow. Surely this man would have mercy . . . But when he saw her at the door, he swore and ordered her off his land. Before complying, she begged for word of her seven children.

"They're dead," he stated crassly. "No Tutsi are still alive around here."

This broke Beata. No longer trying to hide, she walked the roads, screaming, "My children, oh my children!"

She came to a roadblock. One of the sentries whacked her with the side of his machete, jeering, "Go get killed somewhere else."

She passed some women hoeing a field. They pelted her with stones. But she was oblivious to pain and never paused in her lament, "My children, my children!"

Beata walked straight into the house of the local genocide organizer. He and his wife, sitting in their living room, looked up in alarm as she entered, still wailing.

"My children are dead," Beata cried. "Now kill me too!"

"How come you're alive?" the man exclaimed, checking a register on his desk. "You're recorded here as dead."

At that, his wife grabbed his shoulder and shook him hysterically. "The Tutsi rebels are close – they'll sweep through any day now," she shrieked. "But if they find us hiding Beata, they might spare us."

Her husband stared at her, then nodded assent.

Beata and Lambert's "hostess" gave them food, milk, and clean clothes, then made them comfortable in the guest room. And so Beata spent some of the last days of the genocide in the home of one of its worst instigators.

The following days are difficult for Beata to remember. She recalls deafening chaos – the boom of explosions, rattling machine-gun fire, shouts, and pounding footsteps – but her mind was numb.

When the world went silent, she remained where she was, listless, uncaring. After many hours, hearing nothing but the bleating of a goat, she finally roused herself to look for water. With Lambert on her back as always, she stepped out into the sunshine.

Two soldiers, warily scouting the street, halted at sight of Beata. "Hands up!" one commanded. Looking her over suspiciously, they asked why she hadn't fled with everyone else.

"If you are killers, kill me," she said woodenly. "If you're not killers, save me."

"We are not killers," the older one replied. "We're RPF."

At that, Beata snapped. "Why didn't you come sooner?" she lashed. "Why did you wait till my children were dead?"

All the people she had seen murdered passed before her mind, and she started naming them, name after name.

"You're too late!" she ranted.

"Stop saying that!" the younger soldier fired back.

The soldiers took Beata to Bugesera with other survivors they had rescued. She stayed three weeks, until everyone was told it was safe to go home. Beata, however, knew she would be in acute danger in Nyanza. She had witnessed too many murders and knew the names of too many killers. In any case, she could not stomach the thought of living with neighbors who had betrayed her family to death and tried to hunt her down. So she took Lambert to Kigali, where she would be anonymous.

The genocide had ended, but Beata's nightmare existence had not. "I could not sleep," she told me. "Day and night were the same. No family, no friends, nothing."

Finally the last of her courage trickled away. Two years had passed since the genocide, but life held no hope or promise. It was time to end it, she decided one morning, and she turned her steps toward a bridge over the Nyabarongo River. Lambert, now three years old, was again on her back; she would not leave him behind in this wicked world. The water was deep and swift, Beata knew. When she jumped, death would take them both quickly.

But although Beata had given up on God, God had not given up on her. As she neared the bridge, another woman was approaching from the other side. It was Drocella Nduwimana. Recognizing the despair in Beata's eyes, Drocella took her by the arm. "I know where you can get help," she said.

With that, she steered Beata to Solace Ministries, a few blocks away. Several widows were working at the center that morning. As soon as Beata found herself among them, she broke down. The other women wept too. It was overwhelming for Beata to discover, at last, that she was not alone – that others were aching like her, and with her, and that strength came from being together.

Beata poured out her pain, describing every person she had lost and every horror she had seen and heard. It took a long time. When she stopped speaking and sobbing, one of the Solace staff assured her that this was not the end – that there is life after death, and she would meet her loved ones again.

It seemed to Beata that the darkness was lifting at last. For the first time in two years, she had connected with other souls and started believing there might be a future to look forward to. Because the women at Solace seemed like sisters, Beata kept returning. Every time she wept with others – over their grief as well as her own – life brightened a little more. She felt she had discovered a new family. "I started to become a human being again."

Beata still had the tattered Bible that had twice saved her life. Now she absorbed its contents, reading of men and women of faith – Joseph, Job, Ruth, Stephen – who had triumphed in trouble.

Most of all, she drank in everything the Bible told about Jesus. At the heart of it all was his cross, where, Beata felt certain, he had held out against every demon in Satan's empire. He had suffered the torment of each human being – past, present, and future. Yes, hers too. Like her, Jesus had felt forsaken by God. Her whole being responded; she was flooded with overpowering love. "I received Jesus into my heart," Beata told me. "He became my Lord and my refuge, and he lifted my burdens."

She rejoiced over his resurrection, certain that his victory over death had been won for our whole planet – including Rwanda. "Jesus is on the throne of my heart!" she declared.

With hope came health. "I started sleeping properly, for the first time in two years," she said.

Then came another miracle. Unbeknownst to her, two of her older children, a son and a daughter, had escaped death; now, after a long search, they found their mother. Both were traumatized, having witnessed too many cruelties. But they were alive.

With renewed faith, Beata plunged into the task of supporting her hurting children, whom she felt God had given back to her from death. She also adopted six orphans, whom she loved and cared for as her own.

THE FELLOWSHIP on our trip to and from Kenya was so strengthening that we four decided to spend every Friday evening together. Although we each gave our time supporting others, we were very vulnerable ourselves. Our small weekly gathering would give us strength to keep reaching out.

We met at Beata's house. One such evening, rain began to fall. "What does that matter?" Beata exclaimed. "If we suffered in the rain, why shouldn't we praise God in the rain?"

So we danced and sang until the rain stopped and the moon broke through between dark clouds. Beata brought out her Bible and opened to Zechariah. "This is what the Lord Almighty says," she read, "'The fasts of the fourth, fifth, seventh, and tenth months will become joyful and glad occasions and happy festivals for Judah.'"

"See," Beata said, "this was written for us. The fourth month is April, when our sorrows began. The seventh month is July, when the genocide ceased."

She read on: "In those days ten people from all languages and nations will take firm hold of one Jew by the hem of his robe and say, 'Let us go with you, because we have heard that God is with you.'"

"That's us," Beata spoke with confidence. "People will come from all over the world to see that God is with us in Rwanda!"

16

A Time to Heal

FOR SEVEN YEARS after the genocide, my soul had seemed
numb. I was just enduring, existing for my children and watching,
waiting for my husband. I pulled myself together during the day
to function at home, at work, and around other people. But every
night, I fell apart. After crying myself to sleep, I would either be
plagued by nightmares or dream that Charles was alive, before
waking to gray reality yet again.

After seven years, I realized it was time to acknowledge that
Charles was dead. Not knowing what he had suffered, how he had
been killed, or what had happened to his body were quandaries I
would probably carry the rest of my life. Accepting uncertainty was
extremely difficult, and admitting his death reopened my pain. I
wept long and hard. But my tears brought release.

Friends had started dropping hints about marriage. "You are
still young and attractive, Denise," one would say, or "You need
companionship; you need a man to help you raise your sons." Their

suggestions hurt, as if they were probing a raw abscess or pressing a painful bruise.

"If God wants me to remarry, he will send the right man," I always replied. "But I will not look for one."

I was not interested in remarriage. I had found my calling and did not want anything or anyone to distract me.

My mother was particularly persistent, however. "I pray every day for you to marry again, Denise," she said.

"If I take another husband," I responded, trying to end this conversation, "he must be someone who loves my children, someone who helps me care for widows and orphans, someone who can understand my pain and grieve with me." I did not think there was such a man.

In 2001, my mother-in-law made the six-hour bus trip from Mukoma to visit Petit, Christian, Charles-Vital, and me in the capital. Since seven of her sons had been killed, these grandsons were all the more precious to her. She appreciated Evelyn too. She and I spent long stretches of time just watching the children, sometimes in silence, sometimes talking.

During her week-long stay, I took Consoletia along to several meetings and home visits. She observed the restoration many Kigali survivors were finding, through sharing their sorrows and encouraging each other.

Touched by the harmony among us, she said, "My daughter, when I return to Mukoma, I will tell my neighbors to stop drinking and to rather support each other, as you and your friends do here."

My mother-in-law's words gave me pause. What she had noted was true: solidarity among us widows was uplifting. Now I realized that through sharing others' pain – caring about *their* lives, *their* families, *their* futures – my own soul had started to heal. Sustaining others brought purpose, and with purpose came joy.

Seven years seems to be a cycle in God's timing. In the Bible, even the land is meant to be restored after seven years. So it was for me, and I always look back on 2001 as a year of healing.

As my deadened spirit revived, I felt an increasing urge to give all my time and energy to support hurting survivors. In 2003, I told my parents I wanted to quit my job to work full-time for Solace Ministries.

"Are you certain this is God's will?" they questioned. When I assured them that I had prayed about it, they supported my decision.

My colleagues thought differently. They could not believe I would relinquish the security of my contract, after sixteen years with Cimerwa. The company provided full health insurance for my family, as well as my regular salary and the use of a car and driver.

The director called me in. "Are you sure you want to resign, Denise?" he asked.

"Yes, I'm sure."

"Are there problems at your workplace?"

"No, no problems."

I tried to explain, but I knew he would never fully understand. It was a step in faith. The One who had protected my sons and me through the hundred days in hell could be trusted to provide for us into the future. My heart felt lighter as I walked away from Cimerwa.

The comradeship at Solace went deep. We had a cause to live for: guiding others toward the healing each of us had found. Repeatedly witnessing the miracle of new life gave us courage to hear yet more atrocious stories and continue the enormous task of mending Rwanda's torn society. In the years since, our team's lives have diverged, yet I believe each of us is still carrying this work forward in some way.

I became the field leader, responsible for determining where survivors' meetings were needed, organizing these sessions, and then leading them with Beata and several volunteers. We made day trips to forty-two groups across Rwanda, with usually about two hundred survivors in each.

In every province, we met people whose respect for themselves and trust toward others had been utterly destroyed. Some could barely perform day-to-day tasks. Nearly all were destitute. In some regions, every Tutsi home had been demolished; in others, even though the houses were still intact, survivors did not dare to go home – they couldn't face revisiting the site of their trauma, or were paranoid that treacherous neighbors still lay in wait.

Those with AIDS needed medical attention as well as comfort, so our two nurses and lab technician conducted HIV tests. Our driver, a former RPF soldier, sang and danced at the gatherings, inviting everyone to join in.

To open each meeting, one of our volunteers would tell her story. Some may think, "Wouldn't it be better to forget the past?" But hearing details of our trauma emboldened these survivors to speak out their own. Most were still chained to their genocide experiences. As well as hatred and grief, many carried shame about what had been done to them, what they themselves had done, or how they had failed to protect their loved ones.

I often asked Jeanne to share her story. This served a double purpose. In her, hundreds of women saw someone who had risen above the burdens pressing them down. And for Jeanne, helping others gave meaning to her suffering.

I had first noticed her at one of our Kigali meetings. Although this had been a small gathering of women only, when Jeanne had stood to speak, she could not utter a word. Realizing she was deeply troubled, I offered to accompany her home. After walking for half an hour, we arrived, and she invited me into the hovel where she lived alone. Even here, Jeanne could hardly talk. I stayed several hours. Gradually, I was able to follow her stammering speech and piece together her story.

I learned that she and I were the same age. Her husband and her five young children, including twins, had been killed in the genocide. She had been raped and beaten.

Ever since, she had kept to herself. She had never attended a wedding or any other social function, because of her extreme anxiety and because everything seemed meaningless.

Jeanne and I kept meeting, in her home or mine. Whenever she came to our house, my children welcomed her as an honored guest. Bit by bit, I saw a trace of light coming into her eyes. Through many visits, back and forth, I slowly gained her trust.

I told Jeanne about our trips into the field and asked if she would be willing to join our team, to encourage other women hurting in similar ways. I wanted her to meet others, to break her loneliness. Eventually, she worked up courage to join one of our trips.

When we arrived at our destination, I lost sight of Jeanne. When she reappeared, I was startled to see that she was dressed in a lovely *mushanana*. I had no time to question her, however, as it was time for me to address the gathered survivors.

When I sat down, Jeanne got to her feet.

Without stuttering, she said, "I am here to tell you that it is possible to wear the *mushanana* again, to be an honored guest, and to participate in society once more. The killers treated us like dirt. But we are not under their feet, where they expected us to stay. We are not slaves. We are rising. We deserve life and hope."

Beside me, Beata whispered, "Denise, you planted a seed, the tree grew, and now you eat its fruit." Yes, seeing Jeanne standing strong in her beautiful gown filled me with triumph and joy. Our people had been despised and abused, but we were regaining our dignity. We are not cockroaches. We are human!

At the end of each such gathering, our team would urge the group to continue meeting on their own, hoping they could care for each other rather than depending on us.

Afterward, Beata and I invited women to personal conversation. We never knew what we would hear. A weeping mother might need to speak out tormenting memories – or she might simply have to tell someone, "Today would have been my son's birthday."

Beata's focus was bereavement counseling. My main role was with those who had been raped. I listened to girls who had been nine, ten, or eleven years old when they were violated; the youngest I worked with had been only four. Some women had even been raped by French soldiers, in Nyarushishi Refugee Camp.

Sometimes Beata and I went home with one or another, to learn more or to assess practical needs. I made a list of these for the home team. When we returned to Kigali, we continued to pray for the people we had met.

One memorable trip, in 2007, took us west to Bisesero, my mother's home area. We were not far from my father's ancestral home as well. From our gathering spot, I could see Mount Kizenga, Tateh Ephraim's birthplace. Seven hundred survivors gathered, the remnant of our people in this hilly pastureland that had been populated almost exclusively by Tutsi.

The Bisesero survivors told us they had fought for two weeks after they were first attacked on April 9, 1994. There had been massacres in the hospital, school, and church, but survivors had moved together to defend themselves. Spears, sticks, and stones were their only weapons, yet they had held their own till the end of April. Then there had been two weeks of quiet.

The lull did not mean their attackers had given up, however. The extremist Hutu regime called on Interahamwe from the whole country to quell Bisesero's resistance. On May 13, they converged on the region in twenty or more buses, as well as pickups and trucks. Yussuf Munyakazi led the Bugarama contingent, traveling three hours to join the onslaught.

As survivors heard the approaching engines – a foreign sound in this place of rushing streams and crying birds – and saw their grassy hillsides crawling with at least twelve hundred Intera-hamwe, soldiers, and police, they all rushed to a long rocky ridge called Muyira. Here the women and children collected piles of stones for the men to fight with. As the men were felled, women took their places.

For two days, in spite of heavy casualties, they managed to keep the raid at bay; but ultimately they were no match for the mortars, grenades, machine guns, machetes, and clubs of their attackers, and everyone was mown down. A few managed to hide in caves; others, injured in the grass, were passed over as dead.

BACK AT SOLACE MINISTRIES' OFFICE, I kept records of our trips, organized home visits, wrote meeting reports, and main-tained contact with other organizations. After the genocide, many grassroots organizations like ours had sprung up. These were often supported by AVEGA and IBUKA, government-sponsored agen-cies, and by international groups such as SURF, Comfort Rwanda, and World Vision.

In 2008, Anne-Marie de Brouwer and her colleagues visited from the Netherlands. Dr. de Brouwer, a professor of international criminal law, wanted to document crimes against Tutsi women. She approached Solace Ministries for information, so I introduced her to some of the women and girls I had been working with. On return to the Netherlands, she and her team published *The Men Who Killed Me*, featuring seventeen of these people.

I invited a few of the international visitors to join our Friday evening gatherings. Callum Henderson was one. He had joined our field visit to Bisesero and had been moved by the account we heard there. Callum came from Scotland, and I saw his love and compassion for survivors when he cycled through our country to raise funds for Comfort Rwanda's Cow Project. A cow would be given to a widow; when this cow had a calf, its owner gave it to a second widow, and so on – similar to the work Drocella has started.

These efforts are a sustainable way to fight poverty, but they are more than that. Destruction of Tutsi cattle had been a fundamental insult; now, with the return of milk, wellbeing flowed to our land once more.

Dr. Wolfgang Reinhardt also came from Europe, to learn what was happening in Rwanda in the wake of the genocide. Returning home, he won the support of German Christians for our work. The Solace widows called such visitors our "brothers and sisters" – and when Wolfgang later married me, they called him their "brother-in-law."

Wolfgang had first come to Rwanda in 1997 to attend a conference in Gahini, on Lake Muhazi. There he had experienced spiritual renewal, and after that he kept returning to Rwanda. I introduced him to helpful contacts, and he invited some of us widows to Europe to talk about our work. On the tenth anniversary of the genocide – and again on the fifteenth and twentieth – Wolfgang brought more survivors to Europe. As they addressed the German parliament and other European audiences, they realized they had something special to give; they were not just recipients of aid.

As Wolfgang and I got better acquainted, we came to believe we could serve more fully together than alone. Here truly was someone who loved my children and understood my pain, grieved with me, and helped me care for widows and orphans – the man I had thought did not exist.

I knew he and I would make a good team. In 2006, he started bringing groups of Europeans to Rwanda, to build their respect for what survivors were achieving. I would tell them my story, and Wolfgang, who has a better grasp of English and other European languages, would explain the politics and history, which he has studied in depth, both in Rwanda and abroad.

Still, I hesitated at the thought of marriage. How could I be sure of God's will? Then, in February 2008, Wolfgang invited me to drive to Gahini with him. There, in the chapel, he went down on one knee and humbly asked me to marry him. I said yes. Agreeing to marry Charles, back in 1987, had meant moving from one country to another. Saying yes to Wolfgang meant moving to another continent.

He and I decided to wait until after the hundred-day commemoration period to marry, to honor Charles and all who had died. We set our wedding date for July 5, 2008.

It was fourteen years since Charles had disappeared, and seven years since I had acknowledged his loss, when I approached government officials in Kigali about my plan to remarry. As they had for hundreds of other genocide widows, they made out a death certificate for my husband. Several people who had known Charles testified to his disappearance.

My sisterhood of widows received the news of my upcoming marriage with joy. But Wolfgang blanched as I described all my friends. "What do you think?" he asked timidly. "Will we have to invite a hundred and fifty guests to our wedding?"

"A hundred and fifty?" I was aghast. "I know at least six hundred people I have to invite. I can't possibly leave anyone out."

Sure enough, when the great day came, widows and orphans gathered from all over the country, along with Solace Ministries coworkers, former colleagues from Cimerwa, international friends, and all my surviving relatives. My mother rejoiced more than anyone else at this occasion. Her dream for me had been fulfilled.

Our wedding festivities were a cultural revelation to my new husband. He watched, and participated in, traditions he had never even imagined: the cow-giving rite, our humorous dowry ceremony, and the cowherds' dance. As costumed dancers stamped the beat, they stretched their arms up and outward to represent cattle's spreading horns. In the final ritual, one spear-bearing youth after another stepped forward to request my hand. My brothers asked me, each time, if I knew the suitor. I always said no – until Wolfgang's turn.

One wedding gift, an exquisitely sewn dress, particularly touched me. I considered it a symbol of triumph, knowing there was determination in every stitch.

When I had first met its creator, Théophile, three years earlier, she had been existing without hope. Her husband was dead, she had AIDS, and she was shunned by neighbors and fellow church members, who feared her illness. Waiting to die, she had quit her profession as a seamstress and decided how to dispense her few belongings.

Chancing to meet Théophile in this dismal state in 2005, I brought her to a Solace meeting specifically for women and girls infected with HIV. "In this community, I experienced that I am a precious human being," she says of that first evening. "My soul was healed by love. Now I pass that love on to others." She invited other women with HIV to found their own prayer group, which they called Shekinah.

Today, twenty-five years after the genocide, Théophile is still reaching out – and still sewing. "Just as I create lovely clothes from ripped fabric, I help torn hearts mend from brokenness to beauty," she laughs. She has returned to school to study the Bible. And I still wear her dress, with pride.

AS BEATA MUKARUBUGA and I continued to labor side by side, we kept abreast of each other's lives. Decisive events had happened in hers, too, since she had told me her story in the bus on our way to Kenya.

A few weeks after we attended that conference together, Beata received a shock in the form of a letter. It was from a former neighbor, Manasseh Nshimyerugira, and it was sent from prison. In his letter, he confessed to killing five of Beata's children, as well as many other Nyanza Tutsi. She was stunned.

Manasseh wrote that nightmares about his victims terrorized his sleep. Through all the intervening years, he had not had one peaceful night. Now he pleaded with Beata, with God, the president, all of Rwanda, and the whole world to forgive him. His letter was a cry of anguish.

Beata, like a lioness, reacted with instinctive fury against the attacker of her young. "When I learned that Manasseh had killed my children, and how he did it, I *hated* him," she told me. "I pictured him as a snake."

Someone who deliberately kills innocent children deserves the death penalty, the mother in Beata raged. Eye for eye, tooth for tooth!

Whenever her mind became quiet, however, Jesus intruded into her thoughts – he who had saved her from despair. He had lived by a different law, she knew. Beata's heart became a war zone, justice fighting mercy. Her nightmares returned.

Manasseh wrote another letter, this time detailing where he had disposed of her children's bodies. Once more, his words roused all the emotions and all the sights, sounds, and smells of the terrible weeks of April to July, 1994. Beata fell to her knees and wrestled in prayer – again and again.

After receiving the second letter, she went out to search, with other survivors. Finding the mass grave exactly where Manasseh had described, they retrieved the remains of Beata's children – and of 122 other people.

As harrowing as the exhumation was, Beata's relief was great: finally, after six years, she could bury her loved ones.

"I thank everyone who gave back dignity to my children the day they were taken out of the sewage pit and buried as human beings," she says. "I thank everyone involved in building a memorial for them."

Two years later, Beata finally mustered the courage to visit her children's killer in prison – and God gave her the grace to forgive him. He was later released.

"I greet Manasseh every time we meet," she told me.

"But Beata," I responded, "how can you possibly greet a man who cold-bloodedly murdered your children?"

She was quiet for a while. Then she said, "Forgiving is a choice, an attitude to life. It's a decision I have to affirm every day, with God's help. Because when I wake up each morning, my husband and children are still dead."

I knew Beata still mourned her family. I saw her tears when she looked at the only remaining photo of one of her children. Yet her heart was free – I saw that in the brightness of her eyes, heard it in her laughter with the children and her singing as she cooked us all a pot of sweet potatoes on a field visit.

So I listened intently as she said, "My forgiving is based on what Jesus did. He took the punishment for every evil act throughout all time. His cross is the place we find victory."

Through the encounter with her children's killer and others incarcerated with him, Beata became convinced that God wants every person to be redeemed. Much of the murder had been committed by teenagers, who lived with unimaginable guilt as they came of age in prison. Beata brought them hope.

She met nine other former neighbors locked up for their part in the Nyanza massacres. Among them was the woman who had hidden Beata and Lambert only to appease the RPF – the one who, with her husband, had kept Nyanza's execution list. Beata prayed with her, guiding her to give her life to Christ.

Beata kept returning to the prison, urging convicts to open their hearts to God and to humble themselves to their victims' families. "The way to escape your darkness is to face the light, confess your sin, and run to the cross," she told them. "The blood of Jesus speaks louder than the blood you shed, louder than your self-accusation. It can wash killers clean."

As she saw some respond and change, while others hardened themselves or made excuses, Beata realized that receiving new life – or not – is an individual choice. "Freeing comes only to people who repent, and many are still too proud," she said. "Yet those killers who do break down discover that behind God's judgment is unending love."

17

Antoine

DR. ANTOINE RUTAYISIRE also brings hope into prisons. In 1999, the government appointed him to the Unity and Reconciliation Commission, where he served for twelve years. I first heard him on the radio, around the time I left Cimerwa to work full-time for genocide survivors. People were saying, "This man is trustworthy; he has wisdom."

"A bit of gravel in your shoe will hinder your walk as much as a boulder in the path," Dr. Rutayisire would say. "As well as forgiving the man who shot my father, I have to forgive the guy who shoves in front of me to take the last seat on the bus. Forgiving is a way of life."

Antoine and I became acquainted several years later, when he addressed one of our survivors' meetings. He and I spoke at length, and he invited me to speak to a class of pastors in training. I was touched by his humility. He has equal respect for all people, no matter what their rank or background.

Antoine's work included visiting correctional facilities throughout Rwanda, where more than 120,000 former Hutu were serving time for murder. Twenty-five years after the genocide, many have been released. Others are still incarcerated.

While speaking in a Kigali prison, Antoine noticed one inmate who seemed particularly agitated. When Antoine finished his talk, the man leapt to his feet.

"Are you saying Jesus's blood can wash away *all* sins?" he probed. He was trembling.

"Yes," Antoine replied.

"Then let me tell you what I did." Faltering at first, then speaking firmly, the man detailed all his heinous acts. A thousand fellow prisoners listened in silence. "The faces of these people I killed come back to haunt my nights," the man cried when he was done. "Since 1994, I have never slept in peace. I have hated myself and wished I were dead."

Then he straightened his shoulders, a look of assurance coming into his eyes. "But let the authorities do what they want with me," he declared. "Today, by telling all this, I have found peace."

After this man sat down, others stood up – one after another, for four hours – to expose their crimes and express the guilt that tortured them.

Experiences like this gave Antoine courage to keep going, in spite of opposition from survivors who were furious that he was reaching out to killers.

"What you are doing is betrayal," a widow raved. "How *dare* you give hope to murderers?"

Antoine understood. "It's incredibly hard to let go of your right to justice or revenge," he said. "But I have witnessed so much repentance, forgiveness, and healing that I believe redemption is coming to our land."

Antoine

ANTOINE GREW UP in Ntete, a small village on Lake Muhazi. His father owned a store, two fishing boats, and some land where the family grew crops and grazed their cattle. In his own words:

My first memories are happy ones. There was a lot of laughter in our family. I don't ever recall a sharp word between my parents, and they scolded us kids only when we overstepped their boundaries.

Dad regularly biked sixty-five miles to Uganda for the goods he sold in his store. While he was away, Mother entertained us in the evenings with songs and stories. Dad always brought back some treat for us, so I would watch eagerly for his return.

Before I was even five years old, however, our life changed. Gone were the enjoyable evenings. We had to extinguish our lamp and the fire on our hearth, so we wouldn't attract attention, Dad explained. We ate early and went to bed in silence.

My brother told me that the flames reddening the horizon some nights were burning buildings. By day, helicopters clattered across the sky. Rumor spread among us children that their gigantic blades cut people's heads off; whenever we heard their approach, we ran to hide, taking special care to cover our necks.

One day, our neighbor's house was burned to the ground, and he was beaten. My brother and I watched from a distance. When the vandals left, one swung his club in our direction, shouting, "Your turn tomorrow!"

The next day when we boys brought the calves home at noon, we found our parents tense and silent. Mother had barely served lunch when a whistle shrilled at the gate, followed by yells and pounding feet as villagers swarmed into our compound. Dad walked out to meet them. The next moment he was on the ground, our neighbors hitting him with clubs and hammers.

Some of the men came right inside. One snatched our food and threw it out the door. Another knocked our mugs of milk off the table. Clinging to Mother, we dashed outside and huddled in a corner of the compound.

Dad lay bleeding and motionless while people scurried in and out, choosing what to take and breaking what they did not want. In minutes, our home was a wreck.

One assailant rushed our corner, brandishing his spiked club over our heads, a malicious gleam in his eye. But another grabbed his arm, shouting, "Don't do it! Children's blood is bad luck."

Then they left with their loot.

Mother hurried to Dad. His head had been struck with a hammer. His face was swollen, his body covered with welts and gashes. But he was breathing. Mother started cleaning his cuts. When Dad finally opened his eyes, she helped him into the house, where he stayed in bed for weeks.

From being an affluent family, we had become poor in one hour.

We children eventually started playing again, and Dad returned to business. A baby brother was added to our family. Mother resumed her singing and storytelling.

Yet seeds of hatred had taken root in my heart. In my mind's eye, I still saw the neighbors throwing out our food and milk. Every time I passed the man who had threatened us with his club, I saw him as on that fateful day.

"When I grow up," I promised myself, "I will kill him – or one of his children."

Then frightening rumors began circulating again. This time, people were saying that *inyenzi* had invaded from the north, and everyone was warned against infiltrators. My older brother had started school by now, and he told me that Tutsi were being killed – just for being Tutsi – and that many were fleeing Rwanda.

When I woke one morning, Dad was gone – on his way, I assumed, to buy store supplies. The next day, and every day after, I stood in the road, watching and waiting, wanting to be the first to welcome him home.

Mother's lullabies for our baby brother were sorrowful. She became unpredictable – brooding one day, annoyed the next. I blamed Dad, who was taking too long coming home.

Mother started waking us before daybreak, scolding us out of bed with, "Why can't you act like men?" She put my eight-year-old brother in charge of the cows. I was six and hauled water and firewood, cleaned the compound, and helped with milking.

September came, and Mother took me to school for the first time. Other parents were enrolling their children, and I proudly joined the line in my new khaki uniform. At the registration table, a teacher was asking routine questions.

"Name of child?" he droned, when I stepped forward.

"Antoine Rutayisire," Mother replied.

"Year of birth?"

"1958."

"Name of father?"

"Karasira Petero Claver."

"Status, living?"

Mother hesitated, looked at me, then said, "No, dead."

Dead? My father is dead? No, my father is not dead. He's gone to Uganda to get things, and he's coming back any day now . . .

In all the weeks since he had left, I had never imagined that Dad was dead. But Mother had said the words, publicly. I stood as if turned to stone. Then I started to sob. Mother hurried me home through the pastures, avoiding the road.

Karasira Petero Claver. My father. Dead. He will not come back. I will never see him again . . .

I still woke early and did my chores, but I was crying all the time. I would run home from school, brushing away my tears, hoping my classmates thought it was sweat. Nothing could stem those tears; they kept coming even when I'd reached the age when most people do not cry.

Mother never told us children how our father died, but we found out from others. In December 1963, Tutsi exiles had formed an army to invade Rwanda. In retaliation, the Hutu government rounded up influential Tutsi throughout the country. They were taken to prison and later shot.

People say time heals all wounds, but that's not true. I dreamed of the day I'd be strong enough to do something big, something that could hurt these Hutu so badly that they would weep as many tears as I had.

ANTOINE WAS EIGHT the first time he joined the ten-mile trek to Kiziguro Catholic Church. He was impressed. "God must be very rich and great," he mused. "If he has such a grand house down here, it must be something else, above the sky."

His thoughts were interrupted by a bell, and the congregation rose. Children in white led a majestically robed priest, swinging a censer of incense, down the aisle. A choir began to sing from a balcony, the sound seeming to come from heaven.

Antoine went home that day determined to become a priest. The next time he took the cows to pasture, he climbed an ant hill, stretching his arms to bless an imaginary congregation. In 1970, twelve-year-old Antoine traveled alone across the country by bus, to enter junior seminary – the first step toward fulfilling his ambition.

In 1973, however, Hutu students from a nearby academy joined Hutu seminarians in an attempt to drive out the Tutsi students. Armed soldiers had to be called in and assigned to each class to prevent violence, and the bishop visited to chide these future priests. There was apparent calm after he left, but the Hutu students were seething at their failure to oust the Tutsi, and their Tutsi classmates were equally angry.

Antoine was now firmly convinced that all Hutu were bad. And by the time he graduated from junior seminary, disillusioned with religion, he had quit his idea of becoming a priest.

Pursuing liberal arts instead, at the National University of Rwanda, Antoine graduated as valedictorian in 1983. Life seemed full of promise. Set on becoming a distinguished professor, he started researching for a future doctoral thesis.

His plans were dashed, however, when he heard he had been assigned instead to an out-of-the-way secondary school. Making an appointment with the Director of Higher Education, he pleaded his case, presenting accolades from the university and trying to find out what had gone awry.

"I thought you were smart," the director interrupted. "Don't you understand that you will never join the university faculty?"

Yes, Antoine did understand. He was Tutsi.

Familiar rage boiled up, and his eyes filled with the hated tears. 1963, his father; 1973, his friends; 1983, his career . . . He was sick of being a second-class citizen, decade after decade.

With no choice in the matter, he started teaching at Rulindo Girls High School, so remote that the bus ascended its dusty road only once a week.

Disgusted with his lot in life, Antoine isolated himself from his colleagues. In his boredom, he began reading the Bible. He found that it intrigued him – particularly God's aversion to injustice, which he met in both Old and New Testaments – and challenged him to find something to live for.

Antoine had to admit that he was not living for anything. He was just drifting resentfully through his days. As he read the Bible, cover to cover, he realized he was discovering a standard to live by. From now on, he determined, he would call right what the Bible calls right, and call wrong what it calls wrong.

One evening, while working his way through the Gospels, Antoine was gripped by the story of Jesus journeying toward death. He felt himself pulled into the drama:

Singing hosannas, I join the joyous welcoming throng. As the crowd disperses, euphoria fades; only twelve disciples remain with the Master, and I listen in on their conversation. Their mood, in an upper room, becomes somber.

One of their number departs. The others move outdoors to a dark garden. Here Jesus prays, alone, beneath the trees.

Suddenly Judas is back, with a torch-bearing mob. They are not chanting "Hosanna" this time, but "Get him! Get him! Don't let him escape!"

Jesus is attacked with hammers and clubs. They're dragging him away. I follow.

Only now, it's my father, surrounded by thugs, and I am six years old again. My passion mounts with every step. By the time we reach Golgotha, I'm beside myself. These Hutu! How long will they do this to innocent people?

Antoine continued reading, but something had happened to him. He could not distance himself from this story. And when Jesus prayed, "Father, forgive them," Antoine cried, "No! No, no, no! Lord, how dare you intercede for these people? You fed them, you healed them, and here they are, yelling 'Crucify!' – repaying evil for good. You should curse them!"

Antoine couldn't bear it. He absolutely disagreed with Jesus. "Forget it, God," he said, putting down the book. He went out for a walk. "Lord, surely you do not expect me to forgive the Hutu for killing my father. I will follow you – always, everywhere – but I take a detour here. I *cannot* forgive them."

Antoine grappled for two weeks. Finally he took a day off work to resolve his problem. Opening to the New Testament, he read every passage on how to treat one's enemies. He was convicted: for a Christian, forgiving is not an option; it's a command.

Antoine wrote a list of individuals he hated – each of the neighbors who had beaten his father, the mayor who had ordered him killed, Hutu classmates of 1973, the Education Ministry director,

178

and many more. He decided to forgive these people, to "bless those who persecute you," as Jesus had said.

Yet when he tried to do it, his heart still rebelled, screaming, "No, curse them!"

Antoine simply could not take this step. He gave up trying. Defeated, he slumped to the floor where he'd been kneeling beside his bed.

As he dozed off, too discouraged to rouse himself, a vivid picture formed in his mind, and with it, a sharp realization: Jesus had said "Father, forgive them" *while* crude metal spikes were being driven through his hands and feet, his whipped-raw back pressed to rough-splintered wood, long thorns piercing his forehead, his mind and soul tormented, his body racked with fever and pain, naked, before a jeering mob.

Antoine's resistance melted. Wide awake now, and weeping, he prayed, "Lord, bless the neighbor who threatened me with a club, bless his wife, bless his farm. Bless the mayor who ordered my father shot, bless his sons and his daughters . . ."

By the time he finished, Antoine was exhausted. But he was at peace; an enormous weight had lifted from him. In the following days, he discovered that the more he wished his offenders well, the more he was freed from the sting of their deeds. He thought, "Forgiving is not a favor I grant my enemies – it's a remedy for my own soul."

IN 1990, Antoine married Penina, a former student from Rulindo Girls High School, and they settled in Kigali. I asked him how they experienced 1994 and its aftermath. He replied:

On the morning of April 7, I switched on the radio. All I got was a classical dirge. I waited for a very long time, through this strange musical interlude. Finally, a voice came on, and with it, the sentence that changed our lives forever: "The Ministry of Defense regrets to announce that His Excellency's plane was shot down; he and all his fellow travelers are dead . . ."

I stepped outdoors. Our nearest neighbor was smoking beside his house. I called a morning greeting to him.

"Haven't you heard the news?" he snarled.

"Yes, I just heard," I answered.

He cleared his throat and spat. "How could it be avoided, when enemies surround us?" His sweeping gesture included my home. Dropping his cigarette butt, he ground it beneath his heel, then went inside, slamming the door. He emerged moments later with a machete and went off down the street.

Killing had begun throughout the city. Penina and I and our little daughter, Deborah, hunkered down in our house until we were able to steal away to nearby Amahoro Stadium, a refuge protected by United Nations peacekeepers. About 15,000 people had sought asylum there.

Early in the morning on Tuesday, April 19, government forces started shelling the stadium. One mortar landed in the midst of some women cooking porridge for the children, and others landed in stairways where families were camped. A stampede ensued, people running, tripping, crying. When the bombardment ceased and panic subsided, thirty-five people were dead.

The Red Cross arrived, and I helped them move the dead and wounded. When we finished, I found a corner to pray. My hands were red with blood, my mind with anger.

That was the day I lost all confidence in the United Nations. Its battalion had run for cover, their abandoned artillery pointing at the sky like big, unused toys. They had not fired a single shot to convey that this was a protected zone. It took me years to forgive the UN and that faceless body, "the world."

RPF soldiers came and went, disguised as civilians. That's how we learned that they would help any who wished to depart for a safer haven behind their lines. We would go by night, they told us, but they would not say when.

Around nine o'clock on Sunday evening, April 24, we heard movement and whispers: "Those who want to leave, now is the time."

My wife, daughter, and I joined five thousand Tutsi walking out of Kigali in total silence, escorted by equally silent RPF soldiers. Rain and darkness covered our flight.

We eventually made it to a displaced persons camp in Byumba, where our family stayed in a classroom with forty other people. Ten thousand Tutsi survivors had taken refuge in Byumba; two months later, the number had doubled.

WHEN THE COUNTRY was liberated, Antoine returned to Kigali. Talking about repentance and forgiveness was tough when everyone was hurting, but he believed reconciliation was his nation's only hope. He spoke on the radio and in gatherings, large or small, whenever opportunity arose. One morning, a young woman stopped him in the corridor outside his office. "Sorry," he said, "I'm just heading out. But the project coordinator can help, if you have a problem with school fees or something."

He was startled when she burst into tears. "I need to talk to *you*," she cried. "I need to beg your forgiveness for what my father, Gashugi, did."

That caught Antoine's attention. Gashugi was the mayor he and his brothers had nicknamed "murderer of our people." It was he who had masterminded the killing of Tutsi in Ntete.

Antoine invited the young lady into his office. Taking a sobbing breath, she said, "My name is Immaculee. I heard your talk last week. When you mentioned where you had grown up, I realized my dad was responsible for your father's execution."

"I had to find someone my father had hurt, to say how terrible I feel," she continued. "Can you forgive our family? And would you pray for me, too? In school, other kids called me 'the murderer's daughter.' Any time I make friends, sooner or later they learn who my father is – and cut me off. I need freedom from this curse!"

Antoine called in his colleagues as witnesses. Tears filling his own eyes, he took Immaculee's hand and started speaking forgiveness and blessings over her life and family. He felt he had found a sister.

Through this encounter, Antoine's message of reconciliation became personal for him. His account renewed my determination to keep working for the same.

18

A Wellspring

MUKOMA, CHARLES'S HOME, the place with the most beautiful view and the most heartrending history.

In 2001, when my mother-in-law Consoletia returned home after visiting my sons and me in Kigali, she walked to each of the scattered dwellings in Mukoma and neighboring Shangi, inviting every widow, young or old, to meet at her compound. Many refused, too resigned to wretchedness or fatigued from fighting poverty to make the effort. But eighty agreed to come.

When these women had gathered, Consoletia described the healing she had witnessed in the capital among widows who met regularly and looked out for each other. She advised her neighbors to do the same, rather than deadening their pain with alcohol. "When I'm alone, I think only of myself," she told them, "but when I help someone else, I, too, am helped."

I visited her the following year, and again in April 2004. At that time, the last of my husband's brothers, Jean, had unexpectedly died through a sudden illness. The occasion was tragic, but it bore good fruit. All the local ladies rallied to support my grieving mother-in-law. "If it weren't for them," Consoletia told me, "I would never have survived my sorrow at losing the last of my eight sons."

I brought a minibus of friends from Kigali, driving six hours through pouring rain to be on time for the funeral. This gesture finally won the trust of the Mukoma widows.

Three months later, several Kigali widows and I traveled to Mukoma again, this time to lead a survivors' meeting like the many we had held throughout Rwanda. My teammates were appalled, as I had been eight years earlier, at the concentration of suffering in this place of bereaved mothers and daughters.

With no men in their lives, Mukoma's residents were physically overworked and emotionally crippled. The wholesale rape had brought them so low that many seemed to accept the vermin label they'd been stamped with, still loathing themselves, and loathing life, ten years after the horror. Lake Kivu's glittering mirror seemed to mock the misery on its slopes.

When the Mukoma women saw our team's unity, they began to understand what my mother-in-law had been urging them to strive for. We met with them that evening, and I asked Jeanne to tell her genocide story.

That opened the floodgates. One after another, through that whole long night, the Mukoma women shared their anguish. Many had never revealed it to anyone before.

Sobs broke out when the first confided that her four-year-old son had thought Interahamwe had come to punish bad behavior. She said his piteous promise, not to wet his bed anymore, still twisted like a knife in her gut – it was the last time he ever spoke.

Weeping blended with sounds of crickets and frogs, till dawn lifted the dark, and mist rose from the lake.

Our team had to leave in the morning, but we urged the Mukoma group to keep meeting. "Don't give your enemies victory by letting them see your woe," I challenged. "Rather, keep sharing it in this circle, where you can weep together. And find ways to support each other."

My coworkers and I were silent during our long drive back to Kigali. I'm sure the others, like me, were absorbing all we had heard through the hours of that night.

I returned to Mukoma as often as I could. "How can I help these sisters heal from their unspeakable wounds?" I prayed.

"Just love them! Don't let them die in despair," was the answer I sensed so clearly, I was sure it came from God. So whenever I visited, I simply lived with the people – joining their fieldwork, cooking and eating in various homes, walking the hills barefooted, sleeping in a mud hut.

When we gathered in the evenings, we sang songs of courage, faith, and hope. I never mentioned forgiving in Mukoma; the grief and degradation here were too raw. I focused solely on helping these women and girls regain their dignity and self-respect. "You survived for a purpose," I kept reminding them.

As I continued to visit, I saw that a spirit of solidarity had begun to grow. The widows and orphans started helping each other with housework and farming. In their weekly outdoor meetings, they discovered the power of singing to uplift and unite. They elected leaders, and collected money to support those in greatest need. With long poles, the women erected a framework which they covered with a huge orange tarpaulin – a place to meet, rain or shine. Winds sometimes blew it down, but they always rebuilt it.

As the people of Mukoma regained their self-esteem, I felt freer to share the gospel. I told them I also had questions to God, but these did not prevent my trusting and obeying him.

Many women here were illiterate, but those who had attended school now started reading the New Testament at the weekly gathering. On hearing how Jesus had welcomed all who were burdened, these widows started inviting others from nearby areas. They made no distinction between Catholic, Protestant, Muslim, or unbeliever, because all survivors were hurting in similar ways.

During one of my visits, I suggested the group contact their local government office. When they did, the officials were supportive, offering the use of school classrooms for gatherings – a big improvement over the old tarp. These authorities were so impressed by the widows' determination, they started showing their own visitors what was happening among the ladies of Shangi and Mukoma.

THE ONLY PERSON who grieved when I announced my upcoming marriage to Wolfgang in 2008 was my aging mother-in-law, Consoletia. "How can you leave me, Denise?" she mourned. "Now you will become a European lady and forget about us."

"No, Mother," I promised. "God is giving me another husband so the work for widows will be strengthened."

She was dubious. Europe seemed another planet to her. But I kept my word, telling Wolfgang, "I have a special task with women in southwest Rwanda, far from the capital where aid is readily accessible."

I first visited Mukoma from Germany in 2010, when Wolfgang and I brought friends – Andreas, Barbara, and their daughter Melissa – to witness what was happening there.

When Andreas saw the rickety structure the women had built, he exclaimed, "These ladies need a proper place to meet, one that will not blow down in every gale. They need a center from which to carry out the work of inner and outer healing."

I looked at Wolfgang. He knew what I was thinking: at last, others cared about these forsaken people.

When I next visited Mukoma, in April 2011, Consoletia was ill, so I sat on the edge of her bed to talk. I had reached a low point. Our efforts for survivors were meeting obstacles at every turn, and I could not see my way forward.

My dear old mother-in-law took my hand. "Have courage, Denise," she said. "I believe God wants me to donate my land to build the center where survivors will continue to find comfort and healing." At eighty-five, her hair was white, and several teeth were missing – but she chuckled with pleasure, her eyes shining, as she confided her plan.

During this visit, the Mukoma and Shangi widows met to consider how to sustain the fellowship into the future. For one thing, they felt it was time to have a name. We chose the name Iriba Shalom; *iriba* means fountain or source in Kinyarwanda, and *shalom* means peace in Hebrew. Jesus was the source of the peace we hoped would keep flowing from this group, as these hurting people would themselves become a source of encouragement and healing for the wider world.

USUALLY, I WAS ABLE to stay in Mukoma for only a day or two, but in August 2011 I made a nine-day visit. A German friend, Karin, accompanied me. Wolfgang and I had continued to speak about Iriba Shalom in Germany, and many people were eager to support the work.

Two of the nine days were dedicated to 150 survivors in their teens and twenties. They had been young children in 1994, and there were noticeably fewer boys than girls among them. Some had lost both parents in the genocide, but most lived with their mothers and carried family responsibilities – working the crops, tending livestock, earning money – while pursuing their studies.

Our youth camp gave them a rare chance to relax, and it was great to hear them chattering and laughing while knocking a ball around or preparing and enjoying meals together. During the evenings we sang, danced, and talked. By the end, several suggested holding similar meetings in the future. They made plans to get together during their holidays, inspiring each other with all kinds of ideas. Some hoped to improve their English; others wanted to pursue drama. Some asked for Bibles. We encouraged them with a verse from 1 Timothy: "Don't let anyone look down on you because you are young . . ." At the end of the camp, we gave them school materials donated by friends in Germany, to help them achieve their goals.

Next followed two days of meetings with about a hundred genocide widows. We called this conference "Healing of Wounds." I randomly divided the attendees into ten groups, so they could discuss their difficulties more freely.

One group had a unique conversation. "Hutu" and "Tutsi" were no longer named by now, but in rural areas, everyone knows everyone else's background. As an outsider I did not, and by chance had placed all the former Hutu in one group.

Intermarriage had been common in Mukoma and Shangi, and these Hutu ladies had been married to Tutsi. Their husbands and children were killed in the genocide, like the families of the others attending the seminar. Unlike the others, however, these widows now felt doubly excluded: by their relatives, because they'd been married to Tutsi, and by survivors, because they were related to killers. Now, as they found themselves thrown together, they finally spoke about this hidden injustice and the slights that separated them from their neighbors.

When the conference reconvened, each group summarized its discussion. The Hutu widows now voiced the isolation they felt, and the Tutsi widows responded with heartfelt apologies. At that, a Hutu mother jumped up, exclaiming, "Here, with Iriba Shalom, I've finally found a place I'm accepted and welcome!"

Together, we pondered problems that had confounded our people since 1994: *Where was God during the genocide? Why does he permit such cruelty? How can God use sorrow?* Each question led us to the cross, where Jesus stretched out his arms to the whole human race. In the West, I've met people who cannot grasp why Jesus had to die: "Couldn't God have pardoned humankind without that torture?" But in Rwanda, where we saw evil unmasked, it makes all the difference to know that God's own son has been there too.

At the end of these two intense days, the widows wanted to

show me where the seventy-three baby boys had been killed. It was not far from my mother-in-law's home, and we walked the short distance in silence. When we stood at the site, these mothers told, in dreadful detail, how their little ones had been slain.

I felt honored by their trust, but shattered by their description. As a social worker with Solace Ministries, I had traveled the length and breadth of Rwanda on field visits, yet nowhere had I heard of a massacre of infants like this. Their words jerked me back to the afternoon of Sunday, April 17, 1994:

I am cowering on the bed in Cimerwa's clinic. A killer looms over me, his machete poised to strike my newborn son. "You know what we did three days ago at Mukoma?" he brags. "Killed every last baby boy! Made the mothers watch!"

Seventeen years later, here I stood at that very spot – with the mothers.

The last two of my nine days in Mukoma, all able women worked together. To start with, we cultivated the acres of seven widows who were too weakened by AIDS, or disabled by injuries, to manage alone. Our long line worked across each field, the heavy hoes keeping rhythm with our singing.

"Working shoulder to shoulder, after sharing our struggles and tears, is forging a powerful bond," said the woman laboring at my side. "Death once swept our land, but life has its own momentum."

When the fieldwork was done, we built a stable for Theresie, who had shared her hut with a cow. The young people helped, hauling poles and erecting the walls and roof. "We're building more than a shed – we're building a living church," Theresie exulted. "Whoever has food or money, health or vigor, shares with those who have none – just like the first believers in Jerusalem. Who cares if we are not highly organized – we are sisters!"

At least ninety-five Rwandan pastors died protecting their congregations during the genocide. Their witness and sacrifice stand forever. The majority of pastors, however, ignored, supported, or even joined the killing. So institutional Christianity had lost its credibility in our country. But we now discovered that Jesus does not need steepled buildings or religious trappings. He visits and unites humble, broken people.

Before Karin and I left Mukoma at the end of those nine days, the village gathered once more at my mother-in-law's compound. Consoletia chose this moment to publicly dedicate her property to the work of healing.

"Is it possible?" a woman's voice cried out. "Here at Consoletia's compound, where forty-four Tutsi were killed, God is opening a spring of life."

Jubilation erupted, but my mother-in-law raised her hand for silence. To my amazement, I heard her declare, "I want those who killed, also, to become human again. In this place, they, too, will learn to love."

My heart overflowed. I walked away from the crowd to find a few minutes' solitude, and my eyes were drawn to Lake Kivu, sparkling in sunshine. Here, at his parents' compound, Charles and I had celebrated our wedding, twenty-four years ago. Now this precious hilltop was once again a place of promise.

19

Cancilde and Emmanuel

SOON AFTER LIBERATING the country, the new government instituted a yearly remembrance to honor all who died in the genocide against the Tutsi. For us survivors, commemoration lasts the full hundred days, but the official period each April is seven days. Any human remains unearthed throughout the previous year – in mass graves that continue to be uncovered – are laid to rest in solemn services during this week. It is not focused solely on history, however, but also on moving forward. President Paul Kagame makes an annual speech. On April 7, 2014, he said:

> Time and again these past twenty years, Rwandans have given of themselves. You have stood before the community to bear witness and listened to others do the same. You have taken responsibility and you have forgiven. Your sacrifices are a gift to the nation. They are the seed from which the new Rwanda grows. Thank you for allowing your humanity and patriotism to prevail over your grief and loss.

I return to Rwanda every April for this event, and I always use this chance to reconnect with Mukoma. When I arrived there in April 2015, I was thrilled to see that building had begun on the new community center on Consoletia's land. In fact, this partial structure was where the village was gathering, and I hurried to join them.

Cancilde, whom the others had elected as a leader, walked with me. She said she had found something in her Bible that she wanted to read in the meeting, as it matched our situation. Others were arriving too, and my heart was stirred as I looked around at the familiar, intent faces. When the village had assembled, someone started a song, and everyone joined in, dancing in concentric circles while enacting the lyrics: "We were bent and crushed under heavy loads, but now we walk upright together."

Then, loudly and clearly, Cancilde read the passage she had chosen, from Isaiah 61:

> The Spirit of the Sovereign Lord is on me, because the Lord has anointed me to proclaim good news to the poor. He has sent me to bind up the brokenhearted, to proclaim freedom for the captives and release from darkness for the prisoners, to proclaim the year of the Lord's favor and the day of vengeance of our God, to comfort all who mourn, and provide for those who grieve in Zion – to bestow on them a crown of beauty instead of ashes, the oil of joy instead of mourning, and a garment of praise instead of a spirit of despair.

I had been considering what to say, because I knew the village would expect to hear from me. Now, while Cancilde read Isaiah's message of hope, I suddenly felt that this was the time and place – twenty-one years after the genocide, in an atmosphere of peace – to broach the subject of forgiveness.

Despite my certainty, I felt apprehensive as I rose to address around five hundred women, plus a few men and a scattering of children. Were they ready for this? April is the most difficult time of year in Rwanda . . . With a swift, silent prayer, I pulled myself together.

"Have any of you been able to forgive?" I asked.

To my astonishment, at least a dozen hands shot up, voices calling, "I have!" "I have!"

Theresie, Consoletia's friend whose two little sons had been beheaded, was one of these. Another was Cancilde, who had just read aloud. I knew that her husband and five of her seven children had been killed; one son and daughter had survived, having been absent on the fatal day.

Turning to her now, I asked, "Cancilde, when did you forgive your family's killer? And how were you able to do it?"

All eyes were on this bereaved mother as she stood up again to speak.

"A gang of Interahamwe mobbed my house on April 9, 1994," she began. "My family was caught by surprise. This was a couple of days before the main attack on Mukoma."

She stalled, then plunged on. "A young neighbor, Emmanuel, killed my husband and five of our children. He was arrested and imprisoned the next year. But three years ago, in 2012, he was released. Before going home, Emmanuel tried to come to my house, to humble himself. But the village had learned of his arrival and staged a protest, so he could not come that night. Next morning, however, he appeared at my door, pleading for forgiveness. 'From that day to this,' he told me, 'I have felt continual shame.'"

The listeners sat silent, respectful, as Cancilde paused again.

Then she concluded quietly, "My heart had been freed from hate by then, because we Iriba Shalom mothers had been sharing the gospel. Its message prepared my heart to forgive."

The simplicity of Cancilde's words concealed the battle behind them. I had glimpsed the tortuous tunnel through which these women had groped for two decades. Now light had clearly broken in.

After our meeting, the entire community set out on the yearly Remembrance Walk, something done in nearly every village nationwide each April. We walked quietly, in a long line, to stand in reverence at the three memorial sites: my mother-in-law's compound where the village tried to fend off the attack and forty-four had died, the space where the town hall had been burned down with three hundred men inside, and the spot where seventy-three infant boys had been massacred.

The lady walking beside me noticed that my eyes were on the children among us. "They are the children of reconciliation, born in our country's new time of unity," she whispered. "Some are grandchildren of genocide widows, others of former Hutu. They often join Iriba Shalom's activities or fetch water for the elderly. They bring us joy and give us hope for the future."

As we neared the place where the babies died, these children of reconciliation started softly singing a song they had composed for this occasion:

Iriba Shalom, lift up your heads,
Your children are coming to you.
Reclaim your worth, Iriba Shalom,
In self-respect, stand strong.
Your children at last have come.

FOUR MONTHS LATER, on my next visit to Mukoma and Shangi, Cancilde came to greet me. A reticent man walked at her side.

"Welcome back, Denise," Cancilde said. "I want you to meet Emmanuel."

A teenager in 1994, Emmanuel had heard the radio's repeated instructions to annihilate all Tutsi, had smelled the smoke of distant fires, had sensed the brewing excitement. When Intera-hamwe burst into Mukoma in their banana-leaf headgear, he was ready for their summons. Their exhilarating extermination song,

Tuza batsembe tsembe, thrilled him. This was better than the frenzy of football fans, he thought – this time he'd be part of the action.

"Anyone who doesn't kill is not a man!" the leader incited his followers. "It's time to get to work. Eradicate all snakes! And remember, young vipers are as deadly as full-grown ones."

With that, they surged forward, still singing their rousing song. Emmanuel grabbed a machete to join the charge. Then, zealous to prove his manhood, he attacked Cancilde's home.

When Emmanuel was arrested the following year, a new government had replaced the old, and murder was no longer the order of the day. It was in prison that reality struck. As he tried to subsist in the filthy, crowded conditions year after year, Emmanuel was haunted by the faces of the children he had killed.

He was aghast at what he had done. Had that really been him, swinging his blade with superhuman strength, cutting children's bodies like brushwood? What had possessed him to commit such unspeakable deeds?

The death song replayed through his brain. No longer thrilling, it was now accompanied by hideous screams and images of blood and severed limbs. The mental torture was so intense, he was certain hell could be no worse.

In July 2000, in prison, Emmanuel confessed his crimes and tried to express the guilt engulfing him.

There was no way the judicial system could process nearly 130,000 charges of participation in genocide, especially since most judges and lawyers were dead or had fled. So in 2002, the new government instituted gacaca – pronounced "gachacha" – throughout the country. These tribunals were based on the traditional system of dealing justice, using trusted men and women in each locale as judges or *inyangamugayo,* "those who hate dishonesty."

A cluster of villages would gather weekly, at some central outdoor location, until all cases from their area had been heard. Anyone present could question the accused, who were transported from prison. *Inyangamugayo* considered statements from both sides before handing down a verdict. They had authority to grant reduced sentences if the accused admitted guilt and showed remorse. Some convicts were assigned daytime work release, to help rebuild the nation.

Goretti and I were called to testify at Casimir's gacaca in Bugarama. When it was my turn, I told what I knew of his actions, good as well as bad, and asked the once-powerful director if he was ready to admit guilt and apologize. He showed no emotion, however, refusing to respond or even look at Goretti and me. Disappointed, we returned to Kigali – and Casimir was returned to prison.

These trials were traumatic for the whole country. For survivors, hearing details of their loved ones' murders, after so many years, tore open scabbing wounds. Killers, in their pink prison uniforms, felt humiliated at having their acts publicly exposed. Their families, too, felt shamed.

But for some, both victims and perpetrators, this excruciating process was a step toward healing. Gacaca confessions helped many survivors locate their relatives' remains, so they could honor them in burial. And for contrite killers, humbling themselves brought a measure of relief.

In 2003, Cancilde was terrified at the thought of facing her family's murderer, but gacaca attendance was mandatory. Also, despite her anxiety, she needed to know the truth of how her husband and children had died. So she forced herself to walk to the designated gathering place beneath large shade trees.

When it was Emmanuel's turn to speak, he stood and faced the populace, but his eyes were cast down. Struggling to describe the worst deed of his life, he told how he and five other militants had descended on Cancilde's house the first day of Mukoma's atrocities.

"The five others prevented the family from escaping, and they goaded me on – but it is I, Emmanuel, who committed the murders," he stated.

Cancilde and Emmanuel

First he had slashed Cancilde's husband to death and pushed his body into the latrine. Then he had attacked the children and thrown them in on top of their father. Two of them, still alive, had crawled out again, but he had easily overpowered them and finished them off.

Emmanuel was sweating and trembling as he gave his account.

"I was rewarded for killing this family," he added. "In payment, Interahamwe gave me Cancilde's house. I took it apart and used the materials to build myself a home, where I lived till I was arrested in 1995."

Lifting his eyes to look wildly around at the set, stony faces, Emmanuel cried, "I plead for mercy from the government, from my village, and from God!"

Cancilde was shaking with sobs at the report she had just heard. Yet Emmanuel's honesty and anguish reached through her pain and touched her heart. The picture of his contorted face remained etched in her mind.

Gacaca judges sentenced the young man to twenty-five years in prison for his crimes. Because of his remorse, however, he was released after seventeen. That's when he appeared at Cancilde's door.

When the lonely mother opened to his knock, she saw her husband's and children's killer standing before her. His eyes filled with tears, Emmanuel repeated his heartfelt plea.

"Yes, I forgive you," she had said.

Now here I was, in August 2015, standing in the road with both of them. Emmanuel had been looking at the ground; now his eyes met mine.

"Cancilde has become like a mother to me," he said quietly. "When I need advice, I go to her. Before I got married, I talked over the details with her. She is the local official who authorized my marriage."

Cancilde broke in, "Emmanuel is the one I ask for help when my house needs repair. He comes any time I ask, to replace a window or mend the roof. If my cow has problems, I call him. And he knows he's always welcome to share a meal at my home."

They looked at each other, and Emmanuel smiled shyly.

I phoned Cancilde in 2018 to let her know I was writing this book. She told me her one living son now has seven children of his own, and she rejoices to see her grandchildren growing up in peace.

"And how is it between you and Emmanuel?" I asked.

"He's my son!" she declared. "Every time I go to market, he brings his bike to help."

"Iriba Shalom is my joy," Cancilde said, at the end of our phone call. "Your encouragement helped me when I needed it most, Denise. Keep praying – it's not in vain!"

Jesus said he came to destroy the works of the devil: "If I drive out demons by the finger of God, then the kingdom of God has come upon you." We are experiencing this in Mukoma and Shangi – and throughout Rwanda.

I KEEP RETURNING to Mukoma. I can't stay away. My mother-in-law beams as she watches construction of the community center on the land she donated. The building, which will seat six hundred, will be complete before April 2019, the twenty-fifth anniversary of the genocide. It has large windows, to let in the light. Seeing former Hutu and Tutsi erecting it together is the greatest affirmation of what has been happening in this place.

At ninety-two, Consoletia keeps saying, "Everybody, please love! Love your neighbor, without giving up. Love your children, so they will pass it on to the next generation. Everyone must learn the meaning of love – killers too. They need the love of Jesus, and they need the chance to repent. We are ready to forgive."

Hearing the conviction and joy in her voice, it's hard to believe this is the broken woman I found in the depths of despair, in Kigali, back in 1994. Turning to me now, she adds, "You and I, Denise, we must get the message out. I bless you."

Her blessing gives me courage to face future challenges, which are sure to come, because the community center will be far more than a meeting hall – the work of restoration is practical as well as spiritual. Iriba Shalom has started getting cows, sheep, and goats. Perhaps we'll eventually add a poultry barn. Some cooperatives have already begun. Theresie tells me proudly, "I am responsible for selling coffee, soybeans, peanuts, and fish."

We plan to run workshops here for traditional dance, singing, and drama. Children, youth, parents, the elderly – everyone will be invited to participate. We have purchased sewing machines so women can make bags, clothes, and handicrafts. Youngsters will develop their talents, receive academic support, and learn to use computers.

Once again, I am amazed at how this place of great suffering is becoming an inspiration for other struggling nations and individuals. Anyone who comes here with an open ear and an open mind is refreshed, as at an oasis. Rwanda may still be hurting, but we are moving forward, and we have something to give the whole world.

As I stand beside my mother-in-law, watching roof beams hoisted into place to the sound of pounding hammers, my thoughts leap to my best friend, Goretti. So much has happened in both our lives since the long-ago morning in Bugarama when she informed me of the plane crash.

Goretti told me she finally found peace through a dream, in which she heard Jesus say, "Bring your sorrows to the foot of my cross." She added, "The prayer Jesus taught us says, 'Forgive us, as we forgive.' So I forgave. I did not wait for people to come and apologize."

She and I keep in touch. She has a special concern for killers' wives whose husbands are in prison. But closest to her heart are the countless young people with no parents. "All orphans are my children," she says. Through the years, she has particularly cared for those from Bugarama, acting as mother to Oscar and Consolée's girls, among many others – including a Hutu orphan.

In February 2018, Goretti sent me a wedding photograph. The young lady was one of Simpunga's three daughters, whom I had last seen as a shell-shocked child in Cimerwa's clinic, after her parents' brutal murders. Now I saw her beaming from the photo, a radiant bride. Goretti had helped prepare the wedding, and she could not have been prouder had this been her own daughter.

Now, standing beside Consoletia at Mukoma's building site, I think again of the questions Goretti left me with the last time we met – questions crucial for Rwanda's future.

"Healing from the past is an ongoing journey, with many turns in the road," she had reflected. "We forgive, yes. But that doesn't mean the scars are gone."

I asked if she couldn't be more specific. What was on her mind? She was quiet, formulating her thoughts. Then, "My son Kim married a girl whose parents were both killed in the genocide," she said. "Now he and his wife have two children of their own. The five-year-old, Tehilah, asks her mother, 'Why don't you ever take me to visit *your* papa and mama?' How can my daughter-in-law respond? The last time Tehilah came to my house, she saw a photo of my husband Viateur. 'Why did my grandpa leave this world without even seeing me?' she asks. I don't know how to answer her."

Looking intently into my eyes, Goretti asked, "What will happen to this dear child when she learns that three of her grandparents were murdered? We have to tell children the truth – yet how can we raise them without hate?"

As I stand beside my mother-in-law, watching her dream take solid form, my eye is caught by movement at the edge of the construction site. It's some of the youngest of Mukoma's children of reconciliation. Using discarded building scraps, they are busily creating a miniature village on the bare red earth.

Hope surges through me. These children, descendants of victims and of killers, hold the answer to Goretti's question. Yes, their generation must learn our history. But they can learn it in this spirit of working together, a spirit that builds hope and fosters forgiveness. A song swells in my heart, the song the children of reconciliation have taught me.

Acknowledgements

HEARTFELT THANKS to all who let me include their stories in my book: Dr. Antoine Rutayisire, Goretti Cyangwene, Drocella Nduwimana, Beata Mukarubuga, Francine Umurungi, Theresie Murebwayire, Cancilde, Emmanuel, Théophile, Jeanne, and my dear mother-in-law, Consoletia Nyirabiribite.

I am forever grateful to former-Hutu friends who supported my sons and me through the genocide against the Tutsi, at risk of their own lives: Celestin, Thérèse, Louitpold, Josephine, Annemarie, Saidi, and Toto. I thank each of you from the bottom of my heart. Faina, Mukashyaka, Ezekias, and Marcel, rest in peace.

I could not have singlehandedly written a book in English, my sixth language, so I thank my editor, Helen Huleatt, and the team at Plough for your support.

Thank you, Ruth Oliver and Bonnie, for helping to document my story. After the genocide I introduced Callum Henderson to survivors so he could write his book *Beauty from Ashes*. Now I thank you, Callum, for generously allowing me to use your records and interviews. Thanks also to Jasmin Böker, Tina Rabenstein, Jo Emmerich, Linde Nestle, and other friends in Germany for your help on this project, and to Claudette Umulisa, Sylvie Umubyeyi, and Jeanne D'Arc Umulisa for your constant encouragement.

Thank you to the following for your prayers, visits, and generous support of Iriba Shalom in Rwanda: Flora, Jacki, Julienne, Eugeni, Valerie, Honorine, Felix, Arthur, Rugari Joseph, Martine and

Gerard Mukwiye, Abdul, Esther and Dele Oyekanmi, Pastor Kolade, Vincent Sezibera, Vincent Nsabimana, Yacin Iyamuremye, Juvenal Ukwigize, Pastor Rudahunga, Pastor Rugoboka, Pastor Karekezi Charles, Pastor Odilo Rushayigi, Judith Mukasekuru, Chantal Ninkuru, Astherie Uwamariya, Agnes Gaju, Bernard Mapendano, Jeannette Mutoni, Alphonsine Uwimana, Ariane, Kirezi, Gatari Vital, Jacques Rusirare, and Anne Marie de Brouwer. All my many dear friends not mentioned here, I thank you too.

I am grateful to my friends in Germany for your support of my mission through Iriba Shalom International, especially the Free Evangelical Church of Kassel (my church), the Bruderhof Communities, Brunhilde and Dankwart Horsch, the Uschi family, Samuel Hahn, Harry Hahn, Frank Paul, Edzart and Miriam Sinning, Claudia and Andreas Steuer, Anne, Martin, Simon and Inga Mittelbach, Hartmut Krause, Pascal and Rebecca Heberlein, Ute and Erhard Einloft, Margarete Roth, Elisabeth Tabea, Thanh Hah Tran, Hans Christian, Helga Joshi, Kevin Hüvelmann, Andrea Hudi, Sylvie Goseberg, Qiao Li, Iman and Hilal, Irmgard and Oscar Achenbach, Barbara and Andreas Claus, Bettina and Wolfgang Weihofen, Stephanie Isliker, Silas, Monika and Jürgen Meier, Anne Hansen, and Britta and Jan Färber. Warm thanks to the Pell family (Ian, Angela, and Kirrily) and to Pastor Michael Hatchett and the Church of St. Andrew for your support through Iriba Shalom UK.

Deep thanks to you, my dear Papa and Mama; to my siblings Phocas, Clement, Rose, Jean de Dieu, Steven, Ntampaka, Clementine, Fidel, and Emile, with your wives and children; and to all my other surviving relatives. My sons Charles-Vital (Fiston), Mugisha Christian (Titan), and Niyonkuru (Petit): the little you had, you shared with orphans in need. I am so proud of you. My dear daughter, Evelyn, you are no longer an orphan. Thank you for being part of my family.

Most of all, thanks to my husband Wolfgang, without whom this book would not exist. You share my life, my love, and my vision. Thank you for encouraging me to tell my story, so the world can learn of the healing taking place in my beautiful country, Rwanda.

Iriba Shalom International

SINCE CHILDHOOD, I have been inspired by Martin Luther King's words, especially his "I Have a Dream" speech. I, too, cherish a dream: to tend the spring of reconciliation bubbling up in Rwanda so that all peoples can drink its waters. When my mother-in-law donated her land, I pictured thousands of people thronging to this well of healing. I had no idea how to make my dream reality, but my heart was full of hope.

When I started traveling, however, my courage faltered. "How can I speak to foreigners?" I wondered. My husband, Wolfgang, had his own doubts. "You don't have the level of language needed to start an international organization," he said.

But then I remembered Gideon. The Bible says he came from the weakest clan in Manasseh and was the least in his family. Yet God chose him to deliver his people. I felt God was pushing me, too, saying, "Go as you are."

Wherever I go, I tell listeners what we survivors have endured and spread our message of forgiveness. In January 2015, I founded Iriba Shalom International to raise awareness and funds for Iriba Shalom's work of healing, reconciliation, education, community building, and economic development in Rwanda. To learn more and support our efforts, please visit *iriba-shalom-international.org.*